THE INNER GUIDE
TO EGYPT

Alan Richardson was born and raised in Northumberland, England. He trained as a teacher, worked as a nurse and spent a few young and fascinating years wandering about Kentucky and West Virginia. His previous books include Gate of Moon, which goes some way towards the creation of a truly western system of esoteric development, based on the Arthurian cultus; and Priestess, which is the first full biography of Dion Fortune. He is married, with three children and lives in a large village in the heart of Wessex.

B. Walker-John is an American by birth but has lived in Britain for the past fifteen years. She is affiliated with the Mystery School, The Servants of the Light. Primarily concerned with the Egyptian Mysteries, she has been influenced and inspired by the works of Dion Fortune and Charles Seymour, together with the Symbolist books of R.A. and Isha Schwaller de Lubicz. She is married and lives in a small village in South Wales.

THE INNER GUIDE
TO EGYPT

Alan Richardson
B Walker-John

ARCANIA

First Published 1991 by
Arcania Press
17 Union Passage, Bath BA1 1RE

Cover design by Jeni Liddle
Text design by Pica Publishing Services

Text processing by
Mentor DTP
Bruton, Somerset

British Library Cataloguing in Publication Data
Richardson, Alan 1951-
The inner guide to Egypt.
1. Egypt. Magic (Occultism), history
I. Title II. Walker-John, B. (Billie)
133.430932

ISBN 1-873596-00-6

The cover illustration is
'Winged Isis - Guardian of Egypt' by Chesca Potter.
Isis stands on the crescent Moon rising from the Nile,
rediating and protecting the land.

For information on signed, limited edition, hand-coloured
linocuts of this illustration, write to:
Arcania Press
17 Union Passage, Bath
Avon BA1 1RE

Printed and bound in Great Britain

CONTENTS

DEDICATIONS AND THANKS

A great number of people have helped us in a great number of ways, either directly or indirectly, in particular:

Carol Andrews of the British Museum for much appreciated help with difficult translations.

Egypt Exploration Society for the loan of specialist books from their treasure of a library, and for ever-ready assistance.

T.G.H. James for very kind permission to use part of the Margaret Murray article.

Nigel, Kay and Malcolm John who knew we could do it all along.

Becky Knox and Karen Moses - Hermanas ahora y siempre - together we restore the name we thought we lost a long time ago.

Greg Moses, Fred Knox and Shawn Redack.

Cally, Mitsie, Squirt and Baby for feline companionship during long hours at the drawing board or typewriter/computer keyboards.

Saturn, Titan, Pumpkin and Dixie, the American cat cousins who wanted a mention - or else.

My parents, who would have been proud. I only regret it took so long.

The guiding spirit behind the work - may he be pleased with our efforts to make his name live again.

B.W.J.

To George M. Richardson, for memories of lost time.

To 'Gnosticus', in memory of a visit he made to Memphis, and the strange results aeons later.

Michelle, in memory of footsteps in forgotten courtyards.

Jade, my youngest daughter, in the hope that she finds bright memories of her own.

A.R.

And mutual acknowledgements to:

Dolores Ashcroft-Nowicki, who always did know that ships could fly.

Simon Buxton and Andrew Ward for their faith and encouragement.

FPD and CCT, who walked this path long before we were born.

Acknowledgements

The illustrations marked ✍ 🐍 come from a number of sources, some which may look familiar, others not. I would particularly like to acknowledge my artistic debt and inspiration to the work of Lucie Lamy, whose unfailing exactitude in reproducing the symbolic/artistic genius of Ancient Egypt is a masterpiece in itself. Also, the work of Angus McBride whose colourful, lively and exciting paintings of Egyptian subjects brings the people and places of Ancient Egypt vividly to life for me. I have leant upon their inspiration in several of the illustrations in this book, but rendering each in my own style and hand.

Finally, but never least, mention must be made of the early inspiration provided in the wonderful paintings of H.M. Herget in various National Geographic magazines and books of the lives of Ancient Egyptians, Mesopotamians, Greeks, Romans, Amerindians. This debt may not be evident in this book, but it is surely the impetus that decided me - thirty years ago - to one day do my own illustrating of these eternally fascinating people.

Figure 1 - Kha'm-uast as High Priest of memphis, holding the uas staff and the sekhem sceptre.

FOREWORD

Books are written and published every day, some are good, some are entertaining, others inform on various levels and with widely differing degrees of competence. A few are very good, even fewer, especially in our highly specialised line can be called enthralling. This is such a book. It breaks new ground in the way it brings an ancient civilisation to life, and when that civilisation has been as fully explored as Egypt then that statement offers intriguing possibilities.

You can go into any general bookshop looking for a book about Egypt and be spoilt for choice. Take your pick, there is mythology, geography, historical, political, archeological, and even, if you have ever read Arthur Weigall's delightful book, *Laura was my Camel*, uproariously funny. What you will not find is a book that will not only open your conscious mind to the splendour of a past civilisation, but your unconscious mind to that civilisation's spiritual heritage via contact with one of its own greatest historical figures. At least not until now, and here it is.

Setne Kha'm-uast, High Priest of Ptah, fourth son of the legendary Rameses II, also known as Rameses the Great. Kha'm-uast was a legend in his own lifetime and a legend, to those who know what they are looking for, ever since. The Greeks knew him, calling him 'The Prince of Magicians', the Jews also knew him, and if it is true that Rameses the Great was the Pharaoh of the Exodus, then Moses would also have known him and perhaps would have called him 'brother or cousin'. It is said that he sought and found the Books of Thoth, legendary books of magic long since lost to the world. He sought to preserve those monuments and sacred places that were old even in his own time, and thus we could rightly say he was the first archeologist. A wise man and a good one. Had it not been for the incredibly long life of his father he would probably have become Pharaoh himself. After reading this book you may, as

I did, begin to wonder how the world would have developed had he reached the throne. There is no doubt in my mind that he would have changed it considerably. So, it is this man, this prince of Egypt, this priest of Ptah the god of life who is your inner level guide throughout this book. A guide like no other, for he will take you through the times and places that he knew and loved and helped to create.

To create such a powerfully mystical and magical environment within the mind of a reader needs great skill. Only those who themselves have an instinctive love of the country, its history and its gods could have written such a beautiful and moving book. Only those who have linked their own inner selves with that of a Prince of Egypt, a man long since dead in the physical sense, though vitally alive in the spiritual, could have brought him back so vividly and so royally.

Alan Richardson is known to many for his work with the diaries of Colonel Seymour, who was Dion Fortune's Moon Priest, and those of Christine Hartley, the lovely and gentle seeress with whom he worked for many years. Seymour was convinced that he had once lived as a Sem Priest. That may well be true, who can tell, but what is certain is that he brought through a very similar power in his lifetime, both magically and physically. In this book, Alan has reached back through time and brings us face to face with a prince of the royal house of Egypt, a man who loved his country, and its people, and always, its gods.

Billie John will be a new name to many, but I hope not for long. Her patient research and undeniable talent runs through this book like a thread of silver. Her illustrations are superb, her love of detail and her gift of bringing to light the little things of life in those far off days, lend themselves perfectly to Alan's ability to bring images alive through the inner eyes of the reader. This is a guide book like no other, the river is not simply the Nile, it is a river of dreams, of history, and of magic. Your boat itself is magical, it can fly across centuries as well as distance; your guide and helmsman is a prince, a priest, a magician, but always an Egyptian who loved his country.

Do not hurry over this book, savour it like wine, put it down frequently and allow the images it has evoked to rise before the inner eye and fill it with wonder. Then read on. Let the Henu Boat carry you across time and space into a world of wonder and magic.

Dolores Ashcroft-Nowicki

INTRODUCTION

This is a book about exploring that realm known as Ancient Egypt. Not the Egypt which exists today in the geographical and historical sense, with its pharoanic remains covered by dry sand and Islam, but Egypt as a state of mind, a level of consciousness which lies far below our own, like one of those tectonic plates in the earth's crust which support whole continents.

To the Ancient Egyptian every aspect of their nation was a lower analogue of spiritual realities, the whole being an earthly expression of the universe and the soul of man. If Ancient Egypt had an Upper and Lower Kingdom, then this division was also to be found within the psyche of the individual; if particular gods and goddesses were worshipped at particular places, then it was because this paralleled certain functions within the mind and body. The world, the universe, and the soul of man mirrored each other. Explore one, and you explored the other also. To the Ancient Egyptians, there was not a great deal of difference.

It is the dream-scape of Khem, as they called the land, which concerns us here. Such dreams are expressions of deep and potent impulses which have their sources in some scarcely-explored areas of our consciousness. By analysing these images, these dreams from a lost world and the beginning of time, we can learn to make a little more sense of the world today.

Quite apart from any psychological or mystical considerations, the myth and religious systems of that civilisation left their seeds within the pantheons of many pre-historic European and African cults and systems of worship. There were few places within reach of the Mediterranean trade-routes which were not touched by the divinities of Egypt. If there is such a thing as genetic knowledge or spiritual roots which can in some way connect us with our ancestors, then there can be few people today who do not have the spark of Isis and Osiris within. And if there is not such a thing, then we can still learn to experience wonders in our journey through a lost world.

In this respect the *Inner Guide to Egypt* takes the form of a journey in the mysterious Henu Boat up that river of consciousness symbolised by the Nile, visiting the main mystery centres and seeing how these may be linked with physiological and psychological functions within ourselves. At the very least it will give the reader a framework of knowledge that will teach them about Egyptian life and religion as this was expressed around the time of the 18th and 19th Dynasties. It will also give them the confidence, later, to tackle more abstruse and scholarly texts that might otherwise seem inaccessible. At very best, however, we intend to show how this journey can be experienced, not merely in the literary sense, but as an actual exploration of our own psyches. To this end the book contains numerous techniques that we might, at this coy introductory stage, describe as 'psycho-spiritual' in nature. They form the basis for a fairly comprehensive system of inner development which is entirely new, yet based upon the most ancient impulses. Deliberately scattered as they are, like the pieces of Osiris, they offer each reader the opportunity to find and construct his or her own body of knowledge, and bring a new kind of life into their world. We will show that the gods and goddesses of Egypt are not remote images from a forgotten worship, and often damned to ineffectiveness by the Jungian term 'archetype' but are really potent energies within our own lives that are more relevant now than ever.

In practical terms we have presented the informational aspect of this book as the Egyptian shipbuilders made their hulls: with short and simple pieces that are tenoned and mortised together, and often secured by binding. In this case the binding we use is the active imagination of the readers themselves. By building up the knowledge piece by piece we hope to create a vessel that will have each person afloat within the currents of the Nile almost before he realises it, and able to fish for some weighty catch indeed.

One other radical aspect of this *Inner Guide* is that we have used a particular historical figure, Kha'm-uast, who was a former High Priest of Ptah, both as a focus and also a guide. Whether he is accepted as a guide in the esoteric sense, or purely seen as a literary concept, is a matter for the individual reader to decide. The way to approach the book is simply to read it through without making any attempt to practise the techniques given. Once this is done, then the reader can begin to make his or her own decisions as to how Kha'm-uast can best be regarded. Those hardened esotericists who can accept that the latter is an actual energy and consciousness which exists on inner levels, but can feel no attraction for using his imagery, can still make the journey described by substituting whatever numinous figure most appeals to their own psyches. In due course they can modify the whole concept to suit themselves.

Even if there is no intention of attempting the psycho-spiritual exercises given, the very act of reading through them with some spark of interest will eventually cause beneficial effects. That spark, and the impulse behind this book, will cause an unconscious resonance between the spirit of the Mystery Centres concerned and their parallels within the reader's body, soul and mind. In its own way, in its own time, Inner Egypt will make itself felt in the most surprising of ways.

It may seem absurd, it may seem preposterous, but we would insist that the journey described can become a real one, on several levels of understanding. The reader will have the opportunity of glimpsing within the lost realms of Egypt, and within his or her own psyche, wonders that the modern world has almost forgotten.

Figure 2 - The False Door

DESCENT INTO EGYPT

Our journey through the realms of Inner Egypt must start with the lotus. To the Egyptians the long, graceful flower which roots in the mud, rises through the water and then blossoms in the air was often seen as giving birth to gods of Divine Fire within its petals. It was, to them, a pure symbol of all the elements in perfect balance, as well as beautifully depicting their nation as it stretched up the Nile from Abu Simbel and opened up at the delta, where it flowed into the Mediterranean.

Sniff the lotus blossom, and you sniff the very essence of Egypt.

It was a flower which was prominent within the pools of the countless temples; it was a symbol for the shape and spirit of the nation; it further symbolised the spiritual backbone of the soul, and its potential for flowering.

The Blue Lotus is the key to Inner Egypt; but the lock on the door to its Upper and Lower Kingdoms is to be found within our brains.

As the Nile, via its delta, poured into the Mediterranean Basin in a shape that was, to the ancient Egyptians, irresistibly reminiscent of the lotus flower, so also did the spine, with its central nervous system, link itself with the brain. This is not at all a case of stretching imagery too far. The early Egyptians really thought in such terms, as we shall see. The lotus-flower, the spine and its brain-stem, the Nile and its delta, were all aspects of the same, working themselves out on different levels. And because this is a magical journey that we are about to commence, we might begin with a magical statement that will explain itself in the course of the Journey:

In the blossom of the lotus, Divine Fire springs.
In the heart of the delta, a new God was born.
In the base of the brain, our Future is waiting.

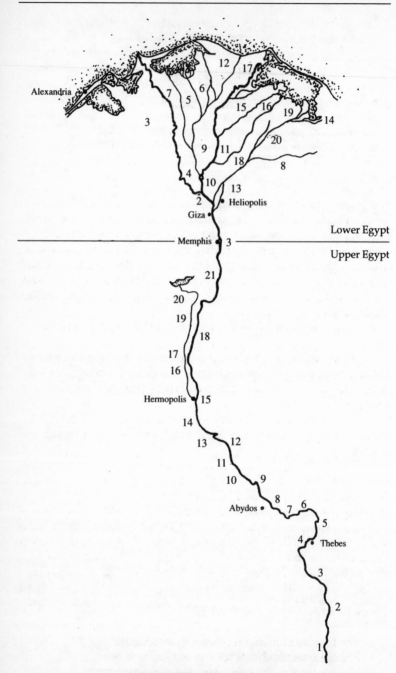

Figure 3 - The Nomes of Egypt

So the delta of Inner Egypt is one with the blossoms of the lotus, is one with the brain-stem of the human body.

This brain-stem is a knob-like mass of nerve cells at the top of the spinal cord. It is conventionally divided into four segments: the *medulla oblongata* (which is crossed by bundles of nerves in a formation known as the 'decussation of the pyramids'), the *pons*, *mid-brain*, and the *thalamus*. Within these segments are the connection of the cranial nerves, the reflex centres for vision and hearing, the relay centres for those sensory impulses which are on their way to the cerebral cortex, and all the major autonomic functions such as heartbeat and respiration. Some of their functions have been dismissed as belonging to more reptilian levels of existence, yet they are capable of linking us with our greatest potential.

The nerve-cells within the brain-stem fire in regular and distinct patterns. This activity becomes highly marked when a person begins to waken, and the neurons of the brain-stem crackle like tiny engines. The adrenal glands are activated: they are ordered to spill out epinephrine and norepinephrine, these being two arousing chemical messengers which travel in the blood. The sleeper awakes, refreshed. In another realm, in the same way, the cry goes out that Sothis has risen, and the Nile begins to flood once more.

The brain-stem, the spine, the twelve nerves coming off the brain, plus the four great blood vessels which circle within it - equate directly with the Nile and its delta. As the seat of our consciousness, it is a reasonable place to begin our journey to Inner Egypt.

★

As was said to Asclepius, in the Hermetica:

'Do you not know, Asclepius, that Egypt is an image of heaven, or, to speak more exactly, in Egypt all the operations of the powers which rule and work in heaven have been transferred to earth below? Nay, it should rather be said that the whole Kosmos dwells in this land as in its sanctuary...'

The 42 Nomes, or districts of Egypt, equated directly with the 42 *neters* (which we can crudely define as gods and goddesses for the time being), which related to the 42 laws in the Chamber of Maat, and the 42 parts and portions of the human being. Long before the Holy Grail was ever dreamed into being in western Europe, the Egyptians had a whole culture which was based upon the premise that the Land and its people were One; and that the King and the Land were One, also. Travel the length of Inner Egypt and you travel your own psyche. Explore the Old Land, and you discover yourself.

It is believed by some that the very name 'Egypt' is derived from the Temple of the Ka of Ptah, at Memphis, or *Hi-ka-ptah*. This, then, became the Greek *Aegyptos* from which we have derived both 'Egypt' and 'Coptic'.

The Egyptians themselves referred to their country as Khem, or Kemit, which means Black Land, an allusion to the immensely fertile soils of the Nile-washed valley; while the *Teshert*, or desert, was the Red Land which surrounded it.

In connection with this name, Khem, it is worth noting that the word 'alchemy' is derived from the Arabic *al-kimia* which means 'transmutation'. Alchemy was known as the art which 'came from Khem'. Many would argue for a similar origin for freemasonry. The innermost, transformative secrets of both were seen to originate in the Mystery Centres along the River Nile. Both of them had material as well as spiritual manifestations and aspects.

★

There are differing time-scales given for the actual age of the Old Land, as magicians are wont to call it. Orthodox historians (who are not necessarily wrong just because they are cautious) place the beginning of Dynastic Egypt at around 3050 BCE, when Menes was held to have unified the country. The Egyptians themselves insisted that their true origins could be traced tens of thousands of years before this when Egypt was ruled directly by the Gods themselves, and also by a mysterious assembly known as the 'Companions of Horus'

There are problems which arise with any analysis of Egyptian history. For one thing the art and architecture made such a quantum leap in development at a certain period that it was comparable to American Indians progressing from the wig-wam to the skyscraper in only a few years, with no-one to help them, and no trace of any intermediate architectural developments.

Orthodox historians, too often creating lifeless deserts by their insistence upon the known factors of academic research, show no real interest in conjecture at this point. While on the other hand unorthodox historians, too often creating a soggy marshland by pouring emotionalism into their visions, point solemnly to Sirius and/or Atlantis as the true sources for the marvels of Ancient Egypt.

Everyone finds their own answers to all this, when they Journey.

★

At this point, however, a clear distinction must be made in terminology. The River Nile is the longest and most important river in Africa, with its source in the immensity of Lake Victoria Nyanza, which lies some 4000 miles from the delta. The delta itself is a fan shaped plain 200 miles wide, formed of a deep layer of mud and grey sand, lying in the yellow quartz sands, gravel and clay which were laid there by the sea in prehistoric times. Altogether the Nile Basin accounts for one tenth of the African continent. It floods every year and the height of its flood, linked with the rising of Sirius, has been recorded annually for nearly 5000 years.

The *Nile*, however, is a ribbon of consciousness - of inner consciousness - which rises from the lost and forgotten areas of our unconscious minds and flows onward to those curious areas where the human touches the divine.

The River Nile is a long body of water which exists to the east of here and flows into the Mediterranean.

The Nile lies hidden within us all.

★

The crucial aspect behind all this lies within the neters. It is sometimes convenient to describe these as gods and goddesses, but the term neter takes in rather more than what is usually meant by the term 'god'.

If there is a quality within us, for example, that is maternal and protective, and if this quality is also found reflected in both the workings of the cosmos and the world around, then this is the neter of Isis. Isis is not, here, some external lump of divine consciousness which may have a few dim echoes within us: it is a great circle of consciousness and experience which links all the worlds equally, from the material through the emotional, mental and spiritual, in all the realms of the animal, vegetable and mineral. This is the true meaning of the Hermetic axiom 'As above, so below', which has too often been given a diluted interpretation at the best of times. The neters exist/extend through Matter and Energy, through Space and Time.

So we can find the neter of Isis in a mother cuddling her child, in the strong feeling inspired by supportive words, in the protective body-frame of a well-designed car, or in the raucous sound of a burglar alarm.

When we learn to create our own Henu Boat, we shall be able to travel the neters, like particles of light in a sunbeam, and explore a realm that is timeless, yet clearly defined in spatial terms.

★

If we can find a modern hieroglyph to explain this scheme a little further, it can be found within those curious glyphs of the tarot.

Although some of its supporters would insist upon an Egyptian origin for the tarot cards, and speculate that the deck was created some time during the last years of Akhnaton's reign, it is in fact no more than late medieval. Nevertheless the principles involved in understanding the pack are directly related to those that we will use in looking at hieroglyphs proper. Nor do we need to look at the whole scheme but instead take one card only, from the Major Arcana, known as The Chariot.

There we can see an enigmatic figure embedded in a cubic stone - the sort of block from which pyramids or tombs were made. He wears a Masonic-type apron on which are marked alchemical symbols. Above him is a canopy of stars. And although his motive power is represented by two sphinxes, one white and one black, it is clear that this vehicle could never move physically.

The impulse of the card can be discerned within the words of Lao Tzu:

> The further one goes, the less one knows,
> Therefore the sage knows without going about,
> Understands without seeing,
> And accomplishes without action.

The charioteer himself is that aspect of our consciousness which enables us to roam the material world in which we are embedded. The charioteer represents ourselves, trapped in matter as the Alexandrian Gnostics insisted we were, but still roaming freely on very deep levels of 'Egyptian' consciousness.

To enter the realm of paradox again, Ancient Egypt exists within our futures.

★

Quite apart from the real or imagined origins of freemasonry and alchemy, we can find a similar Egyptian essence in those aspects of Greek and Roman culture which have, over the millenia, broiled together to form what we might think of as our western heritage. There were few Mediterranean philosophies, few Mediterranean cults which did not contain clear traces of Egyptian thought. Isis made her impact felt across the entire spread of the Roman Empire, while there are clear traces of Osiris to be found in the resurrectional aspects of Christianity, in the cults of the Divine/Sacrificial King generally, and even in some of the more obscure areas of Arthurian myth. Osiris, the great fertility figure, was one of the first Horned

Gods; he was also known as a Green Man. These are attributions which should cause the sensual practitioners of modern witchcraft to prick up their inner senses, in more ways than one.

Much of this dissemination was due to the influence of Alexandria, which shone for many centuries at the top of the Nile's current like the bulb in the tip of a flashlight, sending its rays across the known world.

The port was founded in 332 BCE when Alexander of Macedon became accepted as Egypt's ruler. It remained as the capital of the country for over 1000 years, and was the greatest sea-port in the world. At the height of its prosperity it contained, according to Diodorus, some 300,000 free citizens, and probably twice that number in slaves. Its library, based upon the books of Ptolemy Soter, contained over 100,000 volumes. It was also the last refuge of the Serapeum, the focus of that Sacred Bull cult which is vital in any study of the origins of the pagans' Horned God. A great centre of Hellenism, it was at the same time an enormously prosperous port which helped spread a wide range of culture and learning to the far ends of the Greek and Roman Empires - east and west - as much by peaceful trade as by conquest.

The Alexandrian schools of philosophy brought together many of those eastern and western impulses, and the pre-Christian Gnostics in particular were active in interpreting paganism and Judaism by revealing the deeper knowledge behind both, which only the initiates (those who *knew*) could perceive and understand. Later Gnostics, influenced by Christianity, claimed that gnosis meant a higher, secret interpretation of the gospels which had been handed down through the generations.

The Alexandrian Gnostics can be found today, en masse, reincarnated within the various schools of psychology that have sprung up in the twentieth century. And one of the current twentieth century ailments, the sense that a person does not fit, or belong, or relate to the world in any way, was one of the prime starting points for Alexandrian thinking.

In our present scheme Alexandria is like the pituitary body, that ductless gland which is regarded as the leader of the endocrine orchestra, because the hormones it secretes seem mainly to control the activity of the other endocrine glands. The pituitary body itself consists of two main portions - the anterior and posterior lobes - splitting its functions in two essential parts just as the Gnostics might split the universe into light and dark, good and evil, spirit and matter.

And at this point, by starting to use a small gnosis of our own, we can begin to pull these apparently separate pieces together by looking more directly at that concept which is inseparable to the notions of Egypt. We can start by looking at some true hieroglyphs.

★

Western philosophers, with a different method of recording ideas, use a series of words to create concepts and pictures within the mind, often triggering emotional responses. How effectively they manage this depends upon their skill, insight and style.

Ancient Egyptians however, functioning under a different mode of consciousness, would use single glyphs to evoke a series of concepts. How effectively this was done depended upon the experience and insight of the reader.

As with the old ink-blot test used by psychiatrists, there are levels and depths of perception, and no single truth.

Although the Egyptians set aside, at a very early date, a large number of picture signs which were primarily phonetic, even these were able to function on ideogrammatic levels. The sign for example, would represent the letter M, for the owl was known as a *mulotch*, and its first letter would give that hieroglyph its rationale. But on another level it would also represent, in certain circumstances, those qualities with which the owl has been universally associated: wisdom, secrecy, seeing in the dark places.

In fact we might set the Egyptian alphabet down, in order to dispose of it, because phonetic signs will not occupy too much of our time when we Journey. (See page 10.)

Over and beyond these there are those hieroglyphs which function as pure ideograms. Some are fairly obvious, such as which means wind, breeze - but also air, or breath. Some of them are quite charming, such as which is bone upon a piece of skin, and which can mean exactly that: bone/flesh, but also heir, or progeny. Some of them, however, can disturb or challenge our perceptions, as with the cobra, for the concept of a goddess. And also that strange, griffin-like image which means an intelligent person, or mankind in general, but which propels us back to those Gnostics who felt that this was far closer to the true form of Man before he 'fell' into matter.

We can, therefore, make of these symbols what we want. It is an attitude that may occasionally steer us into some appalling inaccuracies as far as die-hard Egyptologists are concerned, but we will make otherwise dead symbols come to life within us, and enrich ourselves accordingly.

An example of this can be found in the word ⎰ 𓅓 .

Given that these both have phonetic values, then the word is pronounced 'sem'. Now the concept of the sem will actually prove of great importance to us in due course, but we can make an initial and very crude analysis here.

The first symbol ⎰ is what? A shepherd's crook? Let us take it to represent the qualities of guiding, protecting, bringing back, all of which are triggered off in the western mind, at least, by such an image.

And the owl, as we have seen, can be the basic symbol for wisdom, and secrets, and the ability to see and hunt in dark places.

Thus the *sem* priest would be a wise shepherd of his people, a keeper and protector of secrets, the guardian of certain wisdoms under the Moon, who uses his vision and insight to explore dark areas in order to guide those who look up to him.

Although this is a crude 'symbolist' interpretation drawing upon purely western areas of association, the word sem does in fact relate to all of this.

However, it is never wise to be too smug in such matters, or feel that we can dispense with orthodox scholarship entirely. The glyph ⎰ , for example, is not in fact a crook at all but a chair back. In which case we must be flexible enough to modify our stance and dwell upon the concepts of support, of something to lean upon. And then the sem becomes a wise man we look to lean upon, for support.

In fact the word sem is, in our case, a neat and largely lucky example. But luck, whether good or bad, is something that accompanies every traveller. We deal with it accordingly.

Symbols are compressions of experience. Sometimes, if we touch them in the right way, they can burst open and startle us.

★

If paralysed people can learn to awaken unused brain-cells in order to move again, if we can destroy certain cancer cells by an onslaught of creative visualisation, and if we can exert a direct influence upon our internal organs by a developed effort of will, then we can use the same techniques to make our Journey.

We will be making an entry into areas of consciousness and collective experience. The past may be another country, but there are entry visas. By linking our brain-stem with the Nile delta, which

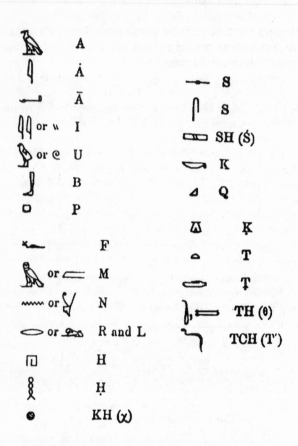

Figure 4 - The Hieroglyphic Alphabet

in itself links (via the neters) with energies that are truly universal in scope, then we can create gates within our mundane consciousness that can help us touch stars.

★

Yet although the focus of our present work derives its authority from the brain-stem, the whole work is made valid by the nature and function of the endocrine system.

Ancient Egyptians believed that commands were sent throughout the body by means of the blood. In fact as far as the hormones are concerned, this is entirely accurate. Hormones are a blood-borne mechanism by which certain biological processes are regulated, balanced, and developed. Some of them also function as chemical mediators between parts of the nervous system (via the brain-stem) and the particular organs concerned. They affect the activity of every cell in the body. They keep us alert, agile, and help our bodies grow in the proper way. They are connected with hair growth, voice pitch, sexual impulses and behaviour generally. By means of the endocrine system we are able to adjust to changes in temperature, to drastic alterations in diet, and to various physical and emotional injuries and stresses. They determine why some people are small and others tall, some fat and others thin. They are responsible for our strengths and weaknesses depending upon how well the glands are functioning. By studying the secretions of the endocrine glands modern scientists have been able to explore many of the mysteries of sex and reproduction.

The brain-stem, and all the spiritual impulses it parallels, may send us out on our actual Journey, but it is the endocrine glands and all that they represent, on all levels, which will help us make sense of it. Each gland has a direct link with certain vital Mystery Centres. The energies that the latter emanate have direct parallels with the effects of the hormones on specific parts of the body. Visit one and you explore the other. Ultimately there is little difference.

★

Three things are needed if we are to journey up the Nile: a map, a boat, and a guide.

The map is simple enough. Figure 3 shows the Upper and Lower Kingdoms, divided into the 42 Nomes. It is, we would insist, a pattern that can also be found within our psyche. Just as animals have certain inherited tendencies which are essentially linked with the survival instinct, so does every man and woman inherit the urge to go up-river, back to the source, and their spawning grounds. One way or another that is the aim of every religious and mystical tradition since time began.

The map in this case links with the delta, the blooming of the lotus, and the complex circuitry of the brain-stem. The simple act of directing consciousness towards the latter makes the lotus blossom quiver, the delta surge with the current, and the map unfold.

As we shall see, the 42 Nomes, or districts, are like the 'aires' of the Elizabethan magus John Dee - regions of consciousness that can be breached by means of word and symbol. In later millenia than the hey-day of the Nomes, when mankind became completely divorced from any kind of inter-relationship with the land, a succession of mystics and occultists, philosophers and psychologists of all persuasions - all came to discern their own regions, and all of them existing within the astral realms or the province of the mind alone. None of them were tied down to a sense of Place, or linked with any concept of the Land.

There are many regions that we can start from in the delta. By means of the Nome standards we can explore them all, to greater or lesser degree, without leaving our chair.

★

The second thing we need in our Journey is a boat. Again, this is something that we can create ourselves.

In actual fact it is easier to travel up the River Nile than down it, by virtue of the strong north winds which can propel shallow bottomed boats against the current. Going up the River Nile is relatively effortless; going down it, with the current, you often have to use oars. There is a another magical paradox there for those who like such things.

The Ancient Egyptians had many varieties of sailing craft which could convey their mortal bodies along the river. These were in many cases reflections of that Boat of Ra which was held to transport the sun through the darkness of the underworld. Boats such as those were commonplace. But for the purpose of our Journey there is one craft that almost leaps into our vision, and might almost have been expressly designed for this purpose.

The Henu Boat was old even by the time of the dynastic Egyptians. Although it was regarded as a vehicle of Sokaris, who was the 'Lord of Mysterious Realms', not a great deal more than that was known. In later millenia it became an object as strange and filled with nameless import as the pyramids seem to us today.

It is a strange, winged craft which in some versions is shown as being chained down. A sarcophagus is carried on board containing what? Ourselves? The head of Sokaris, whom we shall meet in due course, looks out in the direction of travel.

The Henu Boat was never meant to sail on watery medium.

The Henu Boat is driven by Light.

We steer it where we will, as we need, though sometimes the currents will take us.

When we start to use the Henu Boat within our active imagination, we shall find that it has a life and intensity of its own.

★

The third thing that we need before we can Journey is a guide, and it is here that we arrive at one of the most crucial points within our exercise, because we mean this quite literally in the crude and spiritualist sense of the word. Whether you accept it in this sense, or re-analyse it in terms of Jungian psychology, is purely a matter of preference. The guide himself is supremely indifferent to what interpretation is used. Whether you see him as no more than a literary device used to impart particular information, or a living energy with whom we can make links, is not really important. We, the authors, insist that both interpretations are valid.

Quite simply there exists within the Otherworld a being that has borne many titles: Keeper of Secrets, Master of the Threshold, and Master Builder. This being is at once separate from ourselves, and yet part of many (though not all) individuals. The marvel of this being is that because he is a part of ourselves, we can encourage his

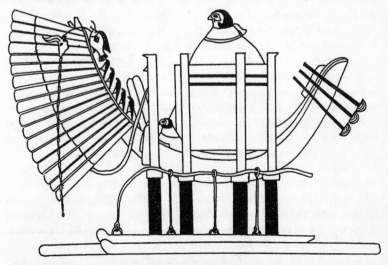

Figure 5 - The Henu Boat

impact within our psyche without fear of introducing anything alien. No need to submit to the specious philosophies of modern cult figures at expensive residential courses. No need to buy expensive texts which use a million words to say nothing very much at all, nor any need to surrender your originality or independence to anyone else but yourself. It is a being akin to Jung's 'Philemon', capable of pushing through insights which are not merely projections or excavations from the personal unconscious, capable of showing us the reality of the Otherworld. Unlike many of those entities channelled today the historical reality of this being is unquestionable. In one way or another he has impinged upon western consciousness for more than 3000 years, his memory preserved in myth, legend, and hieroglyph. He was regarded with some awe and frequent exasperation among his contemporaries in Ancient Egypt; to the magicians of the fabled Order of the Golden Dawn in twentieth century Britain, he inspired awe and fascination.

In human terms his name was Kha'm-uast (Kha-em-waes), who was High Priest of Ptah, in Memphis, fourth son of the mighty Rameses II. Had it not been for the latter's longevity, Kha'm-uast would certainly have inherited the double crowns of Upper and Lower Egypt, in which lands he was regarded as being *the* Master Magician.

Kha'm-uast was a High Priest in more than just name. There are numerous tales still surviving which attest to his extraordinary powers and singular wisdom. And there are those who would insist that he has been emanating these qualities down through the Ages, for the benefit of us all.

Kha'm-uast might almost be regarded as the first antiquarian, anticipating the so-called New Age movement of today with its emphasis on conservation and restoration. So concerned was he by the desperate condition of the Pyramids, Sphinx, and countless temples and tombs even in his day, he used his wealth and influence to begin a massive programme of rebuilding and re-development, emblazoning each project with the statement that he, Kha'm-uast, had helped to make the names of the Great Ones to live again.

Anyone who attempts to preserve the best of the past for the sake of the future, is touching the spirit of Kha'm-uast. It is curiously symbolic that his statue, which for decades was left to languish out of the public gaze in the basement of the British Museum, is now placed prominently within the Main Hall and within sight of millions. As Carl Jung said 'Everything old is a sign of something coming' which could well be one of Kha'm-uast's mottoes.

As we shall see it is possible for anyone to make a link with Kha'm-uast. As Keeper of Secrets he will help you find those secrets that exist within your own self, in ways best suited to you. As Master of the Threshold he will help you across that strange area between what you know and what you don't know; between the conscious and the unconscious; between what you are and what you wish to become. That last is often the hardest journey of all.

★

If we have discussed the need for a map, a boat, and a guide in the most general of terms, then we will pick up the details later, as we actually Journey. And if we might add a fourth, less important prerequisite, then it might well be the actual time of departure. In this case our Journey will partly overlap with the great Heb-Sed Festival which formed one of the religious highlights of the Ancient Egyptian's worship. In preparation for this, Kha'm-uast, as overlord of the religio-magical ceremonies of the nation, was obliged to travel throughout the Nomes and bring them advance notice of the event, like a drug circulating through the entire cardio-vascular system. At the culmination of the whole occasion Kha'm-uast would perform certain acts which would ensure that, in a sense, 'God was in his Land, and all was right in the Heavens', to invert a well-known saying.

In one way or another it is a type of celebration that mankind is only now coming to appreciate: the reconciliation of the earthly and divine, the harmony of matter and spirit, the harmony of the celestial, terrestrial and the altogether human.

Though Kha'm-uast will join us for most of our Journey through the centres of our own psyche, at the same time we will be joining him as he visits certain Nomes as herald and psychopomp. We will explore lost areas of the twentieth-century psyche; he will come to appreciate the future concerns of the world. In the realms and levels through which we will both travel, this sort of paradox causes no great problem.

The mind is like a great stately home, so large that its single inhabitant restricts himself to a few rooms on what he imagines the best side, and leaves the rest shuttered. By making the sort of magical contact that we describe (by even attempting to do so) it is as though that occupant suddenly strides from room to room, flinging open the shutters one by one. He does this not for any philosophies which the in-pouring light might utter (for light is, after all, silent) but simply to study the marvels of his own dwelling-place, as well as to peep out to the world beyond, from as many angles as his windows provide.

With the aid of our map, our Henu Boat, and Kha'm-uast in his role as Keeper of Secrets, we can learn to do this for ourselves.

THE BOATMAN AND THE BOAT - THE ENTRY VISAS

The boatman and the boat appear within the imagination. Which does not mean that they do not exist. In their own way, in their own realm, they are as real as you or I. Like those delightful, fevered dreams of first love, they can occupy your whole being. They can help you grow.

A young child touches upon this with his love for his mother. He experiences her as all-wise, all-providing, utterly beautiful, perfect. That which he perceives exists largely within his imagination, but the reality behind the image is never in question. Hopefully he grows into the truth about his mother without too much pain.

And we do much the same with our inner contacts.

Creative imagination, of the sort which deliberately uses such imagery as that of the boatman and the boat, can open up possibilities and considerations that would not otherwise be possible. It is in fact one of the fundamental bases of magic. The imagination creates doors into a greater consciousness, rather like those false doors on Egyptian tombs where the spirit of the deceased was believed to appear - and really did.

At worst, the techniques given herein will stimulate the muscles of the imagination. Like children learning to draw and paint, our first efforts will be crude, blotchy and apparently worthless efforts without perspective, insight, or depth. But in time, when our dreamself has learned to develop and exercise these muscles, we will be able to produce some comparatively sophisticated art which takes in our greater understanding of the world at large. We will have taught ourselves to *see*.

At best, the forms within our imagination may get ensouled in a strange way. A queer kind of quickening will occur. And while the forms themselves may be said to have no sort of objective existence, that which lies behind them will prove to be very real indeed. A contact with Kha'm-uast will create a resonance within our souls, rather like one tuning fork picking up and responding to the note given out by another.

Everyone must, ultimately, find their own way of summoning the Boatman, or the Guide. How they do this is quite unimportant; that they make the effort at all is the main thing.

★

The basic method is to build his image in the mind's eye, using the drawing of him in his role as Keeper of Secrets.

We can visualise him as standing between two pillars, one white and one black, like the pillars we might find before a temple. These are the pillars of positive/negative, life/death, sun/moon, known/unknown.

This visualisation can be done while sitting comfortably, eyes closed, breathing steadily. Or a particular space of bare wall in a particular room can be chosen, and used akin to the Egyptian 'false doors', through which the Boatman will come to meet you.

That done, and the image held as clearly as possible, you can try to pin it onto the flat board of your consciousness by saying his name, again and again, under your breath.

This can be done at set times during the day. It can also be done every night, in bed, at the edge of sleep. This is the best and also the worst of times for such work, for reasons that every traveller must find for his or her self.

At some point visualise Kha'm-uast coming to meet you from beyond those pillars. In your imagination, perhaps backed up by an actual gesture, reach out the flats of your hands, palms forward, to touch his. Imagine that a slight shock is felt on contact. You may actually feel just that.

It works itself out in differing ways with differing people. Sometimes it takes years.

★

This, of course, is Magic pure and simple. If the reader is unhappy with this aspect of the *Inner Guide* then he can regard this as no more than a novelty, and press on to the harder information which will follow.

But this deliberate attempt at a conscious link with intelligences from the Otherworld is the very essence of Magic, which is an art that we practise in varying degrees, all the time. We have just

~ 17 ~

forgotten now to look, that's all. We have severed our links with a world that was once continuous with ours, when life and death blended from one to the other and back again, as the sun circles the world.

To the Ancient Egyptians those intensely vital essences, the souls of the departed, were to be found in various funerary complexes, always in the West, at the place where the sun goes down.

These places, such as Saqqara and Hawara had been buried under the sand and rubble of a thousand years when modern archeologists first started to explore them. Really, this is a state akin to the way death itself has been buried by western society: a place within our existence which is marked by decay, sterility, despair, nothingness and dread.

To the Ancient Egyptians death was just another stage. The realms of the dead were places of light and joy, energy and communion, where loved ones could be re-united for 'millions and millions of years', and where the living could search for their completeness.

★

Kha'm-uast, our Boatman, has no interest in 'coming through' for the sake of any awestruck group at the tender mercies of any modern 'channel', as the current term goes. He has no interest in what might be termed professional occultism, no time for even the casual drug-taker, an active scorn for any kinds of coercion, or cruelty, or sado-masochistic practices which might take spiritual terms of reference upon themselves; no real patience with the emotionally unstable, and not one shred of compassion for those who will not make any effort to help themselves.

★

We progress in relation to these inner contacts rather like children do with their parents. As babies we have the blind and unqualified love that only babies can manage; as toddlers this becomes an active kind of worship no matter how inept our parents really are; as youths we begin to question - slowly at first - and then break into open rebellion as teenagers proper. As adults we may learn to accept our parents on equal terms. When our own grey hairs appear, we often come to regard our parents as though they were now children themselves.

Man's progress as regards his gods parallels this exactly and there will come a time, aeons from now, when we will learn to bury our gods also.

Kha'm-uast flourished in the years around 1250 BCE. His name meant 'Manifestation in Thebes', indicating that he was born in the southern capital. His mother was Isit-nefert, the less favoured of the two wives of Rameses II. From the surviving records he appears conspicuously in the celebration of national festivals from the 30th year of Rameses onward. The title that most usually precedes his name on monuments is 'Sm', or Sem - often wrongly transcribed as 'setne'. Originally it was a title that would only have been used by royal princes, but by the 4th Dynasty the title had gradually shifted onto non-royal priests. It was in fact an ancient title that he, fascinated by the past, revived and adopted as his own.

The Sem was more than just a priest. The Egyptian word for priest was actually 'hm-ntr' (hem-neter) which means 'he who serves the neters'. But the Sem was one of a number of specialist priests, whose peculiar talents placed them in a different category to the rest. For instance one of the Sem's duties involved inducing trance-like states akin to those of modern shamans, wherein visits to the Otherworld were undertaken.

In his early days, long before he ever became the Sem, Kha'm-uast had had a short career in the army, joining his father's successful campaign into what is now the Sudan, but was then Nubia. Even as a youth, however, he was well versed in ancient, arcane lore. The sages in the temples admired the young man's learning. It was obvious that the drilling and killing which army life entailed could never have held him long. While still in his twenties he joined the Temple of Ptah, at Memphis, as an assistant to a High Priest named Huy.

In our own way we will come to Memphis later. This is the place which was regarded as being at the balance of the Upper and Lower Kingdoms, the link between the conscious and the unconscious, that place where the human rose to meet the divine, and the divine extended downward to the human.

Kha'm-uast had to learn his magic there.

We all do.

★

The god that Kha'm-uast worked with, and for, was Ptah, who was sometimes known as the Opener, and who was perhaps the oldest of all the gods of Egypt. As we might look at the father to understand the son, so might we look at the god to perceive the spirit of the Sem.

Ptah was the patron of artisans and artists, a designer, builder and smelter of metals. He was the overlord of all those proto-scientists within the Land of Khem. He especially favoured the architects.

Ptah was part of the so-called Memphis Triad which included Sekhmet, the lion-headed goddess whom some occultists believe to have had an extra-terrestrial origin, and their son Nefertum, who springs from the divine lotus at dawn. This is the same lotus which was held to give asylum to the sun during the night, the same lotus which we can find within our central nervous system.

As we shall see in more detail on the Journey itself, these should not be regarded as remote and inaccessible deities of a forgotten worship, with no relevance to our modern lives. They are in fact potentials within ourselves; and at the same time they exist as entirely separate energies.

Ptah, briefly, is that capacity we all have for making and creating and inventing things. Not necessarily physical artefacts, but also the creation of words and ideas. His true essence appears when we want to make things *well*, and to last. This is the spirit of the craftsman which we can all aspire toward in any field of endeavour.

Sekhmet is that fierce protective power which is determined that no harm shall come to that which has been created. She can best be glimpsed within that otherwise placid and inoffensive mother who will quite cheerfully kill in order to defend her children.

Nefertum is the actual offspring, that which has been created, a blend of inspiration, energy, and manifestation. Nefertum can be found in every new poem, every child, every created object, every *bon mot* and fresh idea. He can be found in that sudden surge of new inspiration and energy which can burst out of our doldrums and darkness, casting away that which is decayed, or has outlived its time, in order to rebuild with beauty. There used to be a convention in children's comic-strips in which a sudden idea is shown by a gleaming light-bulb within the person's head, and this is a fine image for Nefertum also.

This is a very brief description of some complex figures, but it will do for now. We will meet them all again, and in different ways, when we Journey.

★

We all have these gods and goddesses within us. With practise, with desire, more and more of the skills and consciousness they represent can become integral to our workaday consciousness.

Kha'm-uast, who as Sem worked with this triad all the time, is that impulse within us which wants to develop such links.

He is that which makes the effort.

The details of Kha'm-uast's life are all, each in their way, intensely relevant. They are the details of Egypt itself. For one thing he was proud of these details. For another, we can learn to use the scattered and shattered fragments of an individual's life to create a mirror. With that mirror we can, like the Lady of Shallott, look into the reflections and study a world that is just, only just, beyond our own.

If any degree of enthusiasm has been generated in the reader so far, then the inner contact will already have been made. Kha'm-uast will start to shimmer rather like a heat-haze overlying a solid surface.

In the temple complexes of Egypt the scribes, who were involved in far more than merely writing things down, could be said to fall into two main classes: the Priests of Thoth, who sought to present the world in terms of precept and philosophy; and the Priests of Anubis, who were more concerned with doing the same via mood and atmosphere. There were great areas of overlap, certainly, but essentially they represented two different Ways.

Our present Journey will depend heavily upon this same question of mood and atmosphere - easily generated by looking through the pictures of Egyptian deities and god-forms, both here and in any public library.

In between our readings we can copy these images into some specially-purchased notebook. It does not matter how crude the drawings may be; they are for no-one else but yourself. They help to activate those parts of the brain which are peculiarly susceptible to Otherworld links. It is a turning inward, vitalising the mid-brain and brain-stem generally. It is an opening of the lotus. We learn to draw the gods just as a child learns to draw mum and dad. We do so for the same reason, and with the same ultimate result.

Intellectual analyses and scholarly research are not important at this stage. Just draw until you can doodle almost mindlessly, while brooding upon how a young person 3000 years ago may have done very similar with a sharp stick in clay, while trying to decide whether to base his whole life upon the fascinations of these divinities.

Be childlike about this (which is not the same as being childish). Understand that they were and are immensely potent deities, already ancient even in Kha'm-uast's day.

Work again with the image of Kha'm-uast between the pillars.

At this meeting place you need do no more than affirm 'Here I am. I want to learn. Teach me.'

★

In any sort of work of this nature, the response will be proportionate to the spark. Or what the Egyptians might call Ab, the Heart, whose hieroglyph is and which referred to more than just a cardio-vascular pump. If the spark you feel is strong, but there is still no obvious response, then don't worry. It can take time for these things to become apparent. In any case Kha'm-uast invariably waits to see if the whole impulse is nothing more than just a nine-day wonder. Often, looking back over the months and years, you will be able to pinpoint moments when your life took subtle and important turnings, when you developed new interests or took new directions apparently of your own volition. Only in retrospect will you be able to discern the spirit of Kha'm-uast behind all this, and perceive the energies from him. Kha'm-uast can make impact on all levels: physical, emotional, mental, and spiritual. Often we can only see him through the lens of hindsight.

★

There is a belief in Magic - all systems of Magic since time began - that physical substances can be imbued with a certain vitality, and that they can hold this vitality like a battery holds its electricity.

Thus the items and decorations in an Egyptian temple were more than just that: they were imbued with powers. To the inner eye of the sensitive, they would sparkle.

The temple itself was always, *always*, an architectural expression of the universe. Or if not the universe as a whole, then those portions and aspects of it which most concerned its particular priests and priestesses.

In the scheme of Magic, this particular indwelling essence can be touched upon, and used, quite independently of the actual location.

Thus a Sem priest from the Temple of Ptah, in Memphis, could summon up the essence of his temple no matter where he might happen to be, and enter into his communions as effectively as if he had been there in the flesh.

Likewise, there is a magical technique - in all systems of Magic since the world was formed - in which a person can, no matter what his circumstances, create a 'secret place' within his mind. It can be a temple for specific meditative work; a place of escapist fantasy; or a simple, quiet and utterly secure place within the mind where the indivivual can achieve a special kind of sanctuary.

The Henu Boat is based upon these same principles. But unlike the magical temple, which is always something of a World

Axis around which time, space and events are wont to spin, the Henu Boat is actually meant to move. It spins around such an axis, at greater or lesser speeds.

★

During the Sokar Festival the Henu Boat on its runners was drawn around the Temple of Ptah and also the walls of Memphis itself, by the residing High Priest. It was never considered an ordinary boat; it never travelled in any ordinary manner. For instance it was never in any ritual sense 'put to sea', that is to say floated on any of the sacred lakes incorporated in the temple grounds. Nor did anyone envision it as sailing across the heavens as so many of the sacred boats were seen to do.

The destination of the Henu Boat was quite different. Its purpose was to travel through the earth, underground, into the Duat - an extraordinary realm that we will consider in more detail later.

The Henu Boat was meant to be pulled - or otherwise assisted to move by outside parties. It could not move by its own volition. In one sense it was regarded as a divine being in its own right, a representation of Sokaris himself. This is not so unusual. Certain types of people drive certain types of cars.

Sokaris, sometimes addressed as 'Great God with his Two Wings Opened', was the resurrected god of the dead, of unrestricted movement and power. He can be seen in Figure 6 standing on the back of a triple-headed serpent (which has a human head ending its tail), grasping wings which seem to grow from the serpent's body. In another form, in another frequency, this is the

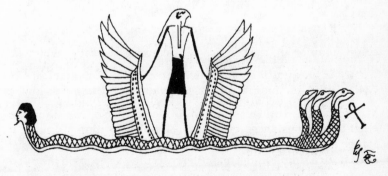

Figure 6 - Sokar 'Lord of the Mysterious Realms'

spirit behind those dragon-boats which carried dead Viking kings to Valhalla.

Technically the Henu Boat was the means by which its passengers could pass through the inert stages of earth - and death - to arrive at resurrection and/or renewal.

We who read this book will use it to pass through dead realms also, and find the energies which still exist within. We shall Journey in a way that can offer *us* renewal.

★

Both Sokaris and Henu can be interpreted to mean 'cutter', and the ritual of breaking open the earth formed a component of the festival of Sokaris.

The sort of cutter referred to is that of the plough, which cuts into the ground as it is pulled along. Both Sokaris and the Henu Boat are aspects of that which opens up, laying bare, ready for the new seeds of a new season.

For our own purposes here in the West (for symbols retain their power through the aeons, changing and adapting) the plough is that same one that we can see in the heavens, the Great Bear, through whose energies we will approach a new aeon.

★

Sokaris is a name for Osiris. It is supposed to have derived from a cry for help which the vanquished Osiris directed to his sisters: 'Come to me quickly!' or sj.k rj. Thus was the name Skr or Sokaris created.

It is, really, the cry that we all utter when we are being cut to pieces by fate or circumstance - or enemy action. The nameless, wordless, but utterly impassioned cry into the darkness for help, or succour.

It is, in a sense, the cry which Hope makes when it wings out of Pandora's box, trying to make its voice heard over and above the tumult of the pestilence before. It is that spirit of Hope which lies rooted in those immeasurably deep areas of the human spirit. Man will survive anything, will plough through any disasters so long as he at least has hope. With that, he can traverse any darkness, cross any hell.

When we touch those levels in which Hope is our last energy, we touch upon Sokaris.

Sokaris is winged. He can fly us through darkness, and the densest of matter.

★

~ 24 ~

The Henu Boat is built upon a sledge. In one of the versions (Figure 5) it is more apparent how the craft is actually chained down. In some of the more obscure references to an already obscure topic, the frame is identified with the sons of Horus - who was himself hawk-headed.

This is symbolism which reveals itself upon many levels, and we will recover some of it as we Journey. But on the crudest of levels the four sons of Horus are the elements of the material world, chaining the Henu Boat in place.

> Earth - Hapi
> Water - Imsety
> Air - Qebhenuf
> Fire - Duamutef

Cut those chains and the boat will enter a realm of pure spirit which yet lies *beneath* this world, rather than above it.

★

The most striking thing about the boat, without the frame, is the wings. On inner levels they are iridescent. Rainbow colours, flashing and alive. When the boat travels they tend to fold themselves backward, and around, to create a hull around the bare keel.

★

The next most striking thing is the closed chapel on the boat, often described as a sarcophagus, on top of which is Sokaris, gazing forward with eyes that can pick out an insect from across the miles, and ourselves from across the aeons. Within this is the Mystery which lies at the heart of every individual. Within this, lies our essence. That chapel is the power-source of the Henu Boat, the energy of our selves.

We can build the basic structure of the Boat as magicians would build their inner temples. Setting a specific time of the day aside when we are likely to be free from distractions, we can quite deliberately visualise ourselves as building it from scratch, with the infinite raw materials of the imagination. How each person approaches this is a matter of individual whim, but they should pause at every stage and (in their dream-self) run their hands over the structures just created as they would a solid artefact.

In a short time it will become real within the mind. The head of Sokaris atop of the Boat will be seen (and felt) as a real head; the wings as diaphanous and textural as any butterfly's; the wood of the keel will have a grain as any actual keel; the chains holding it to the sled will feel icy to the touch.

Before long you will be able to clamber over this Boat in your imagination and have the sense that, in some realm beyond this, you really have created something.

★

Do this now. Have the sense of Kha'm-uast behind you as you work. When it is finished, and reinforced within the imagination over several nights, make a point of clambering aboard it.

See the wings ripple, very gently, as though ruffled by solar winds. Look beyond the prow into absolute darkness. Feel the chains straining under the tension of impending flight.

Soon, soon we will learn the word that will loose them.

★

If we are to understand the regions and regions that are to be traversed, then first we must look at two symbols.

✕ was the Egyptian symbol for the heavens, the Nuit star.

⊗ was the Egyptian symbol for what we might loosely term the underworld. The ⊗ is variously rendered as Dat, Tat, Duat or Tuat; but because the latter is phonetically similar to the old English vulgarism of 'twat', it is the Duat version which has become quite standard. Even so, it would be accurate to say 'the source of all life is to be found within the Tuat/twat', but elegance of prose demands the other version.

We can find stellar truths in even the coarsest of vulgarisms. They did so all the time in Ancient Egypt. Despite the grace and refinement of their art and architecture, they were hardly the most shockable of peoples.

★

The Duat, then, can be vaguely translated as the Underworld, although the Egyptians were never hooked on seeing it as being solely *beneath* anywhere. Some versions did place it under ground: other versions saw it as being beyond the circle of stars; the most sophisticated variants could accept both at the same time.

The Duat is both the subconscious mind, and also what occultists would call the astral plane. The astral plane and the subconscious mind were (are) one and the same. No difference. That which is without, can also be found within. If absolute consciousness must necessarily mean complete knowledge of the subconscious, too, then the reverse is also a tenable proposition. To explore the underworld is also to explore the stars. The way to light is often through darkness.

The Duat contains all things. Or if not all things exactly, the potential for all things. To bring vulgarism to our aid again, then the potentials and energies which can be released by entering the Duat, are much the same as those we can tap when dealing with the twat. Life, love, and the most extraordinary possibilities can arise when dealing with this dark but glistening realm.

The Duat is the place of darkness, then, but it also pulsates with the rolling billows of the astral light.

The Duat can cope with all such paradoxes.

★

We can enter the Duat quite easily, by using symbols. Each symbol can provoke a simple conscious response which has a potentially massive subconscious back-up.

The symbol 𓃢 for example, can make conscious, intellectual links with the jackal-god Anubis; yet behind these may lie subconscious reactions to the very nature of the jackal in its scavenger and nighthowler roles. Symbols can be the thin ice across a deep and very dark river. Sometimes we can fall through.

★

We have already discussed how the very geography of Egypt was an expression of the universe and the soul of man, the whole being divided into those 42 portions known as the Nomes. The Nomes were administrative districts. They were also the bits and pieces of a human's constitution.

The nearest western equivalent to this concept can be found in those old astrological and alchemical charts which linked the zodiac signs with parts of the human anatomy. Thus the genitals were equated with the sign of Scorpio. And Scorpio in the Great Body of God, had a function akin to the genitals in the mortal.

As above, so below - in Europe as in Egypt.

The one thing that links all the regions and parts and portions is the Duat. Enter the Duat from the place you are at now, and you can surface in any of those regions, parts and portions as they extend through time and space.

In one sense the Duat is like a door.

In one sense the Duat *is* a door.

Each Nome, then, as well as having purely physical boundaries, and histories, and inhabitants, can also be seen as a region of consciousness. Each one can be used in the same way a genetic scientist might, in the future, clone a complete individual from a single piece of cell-tissue. We can attempt to re-capture or rebuild the whole of Egypt from just one small Nome. Which one we choose is a matter of taste. The rest of the spirit of Egypt will slowly manifest itself through its portals just as strongly as any other. Only the sequence and emphasis will differ. In a crude sense it will be as though one person began reconstructing a body via the toes, and another via the left ear.

★

Each Nome had its own symbol (see Appendix A). This was shown on the Nome Standard, which was paraded on official occasions in the same way the Roman Legions paraded theirs, or trade-unions today do similar with their banners.

As the whole impulse for this book comes from Memphis, then the standard for that city was:

It bore the title of the White Wall, which referred to the huge wall which once encircled the entire complex. Each Nome bore their titles in a manner akin to American States calling themselves the Mountain State, or the Bluegrass State, often involving totem creatures also, such as wildcats, or mountain lions. Another Nome in the Upper Kingdom bore the title Great Land and had a stylised head as its symbol, a reference to that portion of Osiris' body believed to be buried there.

White Wall

Great Land

Each one represents, in effect, an entry visa to particular areas of the psyche. The symbols of each, whether they are consciously understood or not, are means by which we might touch certain areas of the Duat.

If the bare image of Kha'm-uast can become, in a very real sense 'ensouled', then much the same might be said about the Nome

Standards (complete set of which is given in Appendix A). They are keys to unlocking things - 'wonderful things', as was once said.

In this sense we are back with our tarot card The Chariot: the use of symbols to travel far and fast, the control of those light and dark sphinx-like energies. But as with any symbol we have to work at it. Each symbol is like an electrical circuit, with ourselves as the actual current: if it is correctly made, with proper connections, then light will appear. In this case results are proportional to the effort. The only unpredictable element is how quickly they might appear.

~3~

THE MYSTICAL ISLE OF KHEBIT

In a sense, the western psyche first began to come to terms with Ancient Egypt in 1799 when French troops near Rosetta, at the mouth of the Nile delta, unearthed an engraved stone that would ultimately provide the basis for continuous and coherent research into the lost Mysteries of that land, inspire new arts and Magic, and pave the way for a queer kind of communion between the aeons. In that same year the art of making continuous sheet paper was perfected; a mammoth was found perfectly preserved in ice, in Siberia; William Blake was making his tempera *The Adoration of the Magi*, while Mungo Park was busy publishing his influential *Travels in the Interior of Africa*.

Kha'm-uast, who had spent a lifetime working with the neters, would have seen all these events and more as differing expressions of the same thing.

Three years later, in 1802, when tantalum and ultra-violet rays were discovered, and dark lines observed in the sun's spectrum, and Thomas Wedgewood made photography possible by describing the effect of light upon silver nitrate, the Swedish diplomat Akerblad was the first to publish a demotic alphabet based upon his analyses of the Rosetta Stone, as it was now called.

These events are all simply culled from encyclopedias of dates and events which also, curiously, give the year 200 BCE as the tentative date both for the engraving of the Rosetta Stone and - significantly - the Gundestrop Cauldron, from Denmark.

If the former was instrumental in enabling modern man to penetrate a forgotten past, then the latter, adorned with the Horned God of the Celts, has been equally effective in its own way in helping us to remember a lost deity which was once supremely important, and which may very well have derived from one of the earlier forms of Osiris.

This way of looking at things is the Game of the Neters, in which events, circumstances, moods, impulses and geographies are fitted inside each other like Russian Dolls. Or, more appropriate, like the mummy in its series of boxes, each box of a different substance, each box relating to the next - 'but after another manner'.

It is a game that we can all play, must play, if we are to connect.

★

Rosetta would be a fine place to begin our Journey if we were to approach Inner Egypt on purely intellectual levels. The spirit of Rosetta is behind all those countless books which are derived, ultimately, from that learning and scholarship which is based upon a decipherment of the hieroglyphs. But to approach Egypt on magical levels, as Kha'm-uast intends, the only *real* contender as a point of embarkation is Khebit.

★

The origins of Khebit are to be found in pre-dynastic Egypt. The very term 'pre-dynastic Egypt' tends to evoke responses akin to those when we refer to Europe in the Dark Ages. This was a period, however, which was no more and no less chaotic than in any of the other regions in the world at that time. Indeed, according to the myth, it was during this indeterminate but necessarily vast period that Egypt was ruled directly by the gods, the Company of Horus, without need of any human intermediaries in the form of pharaohs.

Myth apart, it was during this period that the concept of the Sem was derived. The Magic of this period, as practised by the Sem priests, was far closer to what we now know as shamanism, which later became institutionalised via the theocracies of the Divine King.

When we go with Kha'm-uast to Khebit, we enter the shadow of the shaman. Against all likelihood, we will never get too far from that shadow no matter how far we travel up the Nile.

★

The Isle of Khebit was described as a marshy stretch of land lying near Per-Uatchit (Buto), which was an ancient city in the north-east of the delta.

Per-Uatchit means House of Uatchit; Uatchit being the Wadjet (cobra) Goddess of the North. It was the cobra which guarded the

mystic isle of Chemmis; it was the cobra 🐍 which was the symbol for the goddess generally. Only by assuming the form of a cobra, or the scorpion, could anyone enter the isle. The rulers of the area, in predynastic times, called themselves 'He Who Belongs To The Bee'. According to some, the name Khebit (which the Greeks mispronounced as 'Chemmis')   means 'Swamp of the Bee King'. These are references which will cause the ears of certain types of magician to prick up at once. The rest of us will come to terms with them at a later stage of the Journey.

According to the tales, the goddess Isis retreated to the papyrus swamps around Khebit which were known as Na-ateh, or the Natho of the Greeks. It was the god Thoth who helped Isis find her way through the swamps to Khebit itself, where in a sacred 'Bush', or thicket, she gave birth to her wonderchild, Horus.

These are all names that we will become familiar with when we visit Heliopolis.

In the female, Khebit is that place within the mind and spirit where the cobra-powers soar into vision after their journey from that sacred centre tucked away 'behind the bush'.

This is a modern vulgarity of course, of the sort beloved by certain gods, 'bush' being common slang for the pubic hair. It is a play on words as well as locations, but the truth is there just the same. The Egyptians knew that the 'higher' links with the 'lower' via a kind of Mobius strip in which the outside is also the inside. They knew that the interchange of sexual energies is akin to the interchange of magical energies.

The endocrine association of Khebit is with the pineal gland, the latter being regarded by the Greeks, for example, as the regulator of the flow of thought, and by Descartes as the seat of the soul. But it has long been thought, also, that one of the functions of the pineal gland is to regulate the onset of puberty and to control the secretions of the gonads. While medical researchers are still uncertain as to the precise role of this gland, they broadly favour the possibility of a pineal-gonadal relationship, just as eastern mystics insist on a direct link between that chakra at the base of the spine, and the one which manifests upon the brow as the Third Eye. Also, the pineal gland has been implicated in the control of the adrenal hormones responsible for regulation of salt and water balance. Which Khebit, in its situation in the marshes leading to the sea, is well placed to reflect.

Khebit, then, is intimately connected with the secrets of sex and fertility. It is the place where gods are born. Penetrate the bush of the goddess's most holy place, and you achieve gnosis.

On Khebit, in the small place within the centre of the cranium, serpents will fly and vultures will have knowledge of the earth and its ways. The Upper and Lower Kingdoms will have unity, and the aeons will conjoin.

These are all conundrums which will speak for themselves, when we Journey. We don't need to understand them now.

The uraeus worn upon the brows of certain priestesses was a direct reference to the awakened powers of the pineal gland which, physically, is seen as a small, reddish body lying deep within the brain behind the third ventricle, and connected with the optic thalami by two nervous structures called peduncles, and which would been from Khebit itself as causeways across the marsh. It is either a crude development or an atrophied example of the 'third' or median eye of certain lizards and fish.

With respect to the former we find ourselves back with the 🐍 again: a symbol which the Ancient Egyptians used to represent themselves as a people.

On Khebit we learn to *see*. We approach our oldest nature.

Yet Khebit is essentially a mystic location, despite its broad general location given as being near Per-Uatchit. Like Avalon, like Camelot, it is linked with immense antiquity, magical conceptions, the birth of gods beneath the shadowing goddess, shape-changing and serpents. In some sources, it is described as the 'floating isle'. As with Avalon and its Once and Future King, Khebit is linked with mankind's imminent future via Horus. It is the place where cobras are charmed into waking and rising, goddesses find their true return and balances are made to the world.

Khebit is that place which is always and necessarily out of time, a place which floats between the worlds, and levels of consciousness, yet linking them. Khebit is that place where past and future can be experienced. If there was a period in mankind's history when he did have, in some form, the perceptions of a 'third eye', and hence the sight of the Two Worlds, then it is a period and experience linked with Khebit. And if we can, on the verge of the 21st century, find our own way to Khebit and penetrate the secrets of the pineal body, then we can reach the twin horizons of that which has been, and that which is yet to come. Worlds will be connected, harmonies restored.

As the great goddess Isis enjoined: 'Find ye me straightaway a way to the swamps and to the hidden places in Khebit.'

The goddess has to go there: she cannot give birth otherwise. And we have to forge our own way through the swamps of mundane consciousness to help her: we cannot give birth to our own and the world's future otherwise.

★

We can visualise Khebit quite easily:

Sun rising slowly behind mists, to our right. Grey, pearly-grey mists which sweep and swirl above the marshes. Nothing around us in any direction but marsh and mist, dampness and glistenings. Nothing solid underfoot, nothing to hold onto. Only stillness and emptiness and mist - and that strange sea-smell and those strange anticipations that are so much like sex, and its desire.

Kha'm-uast is with us, behind us. He points out an ibis with his *uas* wand, which we can see through an ovular gap appearing in the mists, taking its measured and long-legged stride into the heart of the swamps. We follow, clumsily at first and then with increasing ease as the ground firms underfoot.

The ibis disappears. For a moment the mist thickens, a solid wall of iridiscent grey, pearl-grey. Forward or back, the choice is yours. Back to what you know; forward to the unknown - which is really no more than what you used to know, aeons before.

The moment you take the step forward the mist dissipates, the mystic isle of Khebit is revealed, glistening in the distance, reached by a long, narrow, and obviously ancient causeway which stretches (curving slightly) across the deep waters of an open but very calm sea.

Whatever form the island takes is its true form for you. Often it takes a little while to 'solidify'. Approach it via that causeway of grey, beaten stone. Have the sense that in the sea-depths at either side faces are looking up at you, strangely familiar and half-remembered. They are in fact your ancestors, the bright spirits of the departed. They float around and under Khebit, giving it power, supporting it. They do much the same for us in our daily lives, if we but knew it.

The rest of the visualisation is entirely personal. It is in fact the centre of your own consciousness that you are entering. We should, however, try to build into our image of the island a central harbour, with two long enclosing walls, each one having an ancient square tower at the end bearing the symbol for the eye.

In fact it is from this harbour, a highly stylised reduction of the brain as it exists around the consciousness of the pineal gland, that we can think about launching our Henu Boat, and beginning the Journey.

★

Khebit, when we first touch solid ground, is clearly a haunted place. Ancient moods and modes begin to make themselves felt; we catch glimpses of strange hooded figures that are uncomfortably like the cartoon images of ghosts.

These are the forgotten figures of that pre-dynastic manner of worship which was once universal, and which we would now describe as shamanistic. In the case of the people of Khem, at least, the shaman practices of the local cultures became institutionalised and ritualised on a colossal scale, evolving over the centuries, over the millenia, into the cult of the pharaoh.

They are figures which impinge upon our psyches with surprising ease, if we want them to. As though they have been waiting outside the doors of perception for an exceedingly long, cold time, and are only too glad to slip inside at the slightest hint of an invitation.

Although they are the shaman-spirits of mankind's oldest worship, they have more to teach us now than ever before.

The actual image given in Figure 7a is taken from a bone figure found in El Amra, dating from a notional 3800 BCE, but it is a form which is bland enough to accept a huge range of emotional, religious, and psychic associations. Devoid of any personality through their garb, they are the men and women who once became pure channels for communion with the worlds, linking life and death, matter and spirit, past and future. If there is a tradition in the East that certain great souls can deliberately forsake eternal bliss in order to continue to serve mankind on the material plane, then here amid the delta of the Nile we encounter souls who choose to do similar from astral realms. There is no need to summon, stir, or call them up. As far as Khebit is concerned, they come with the territory.

★

It is time to leave now, and begin the Journey. We can charge the moment with intensity by devising a cohesive and coherent sequence of visualisations which lead from the contact with Kha'm-uast to the arrival on Khebit. The individual must do this for him or herself; as we shall see when we study the formulae of Osiris, the very effort of doing so is part of the Magic. There is no standard or 'correct' method - only suggestions.

★

See that harbour again now, its walls on either side to the right and left of your perceptions, curving inward slightly to form a narrow harbour mouth, a gateway to the Nile beyond. The eyes in the towers glow, alive in the noon-day sun.

The water is low, the Inundation not yet begun. Marsh and waste both inside and beyond the harbour walls, and the only solid ground before you being a large, flat, reddish expanse of rock only

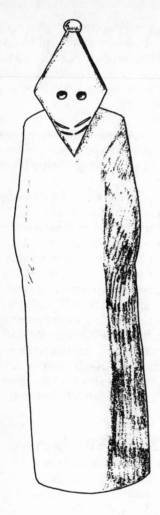

Figure 7a - Bone figure of a cloaked and hooded man, from El Amra, the Naqada I period, circa 3800 BCE.

Figure 7b - Archaic Egyptian 'Lord of the Dance' shaman

just raised above the mud, on which the frame of the Henu Boat is fixed.

Feel Kha'm-uast's presence behind you again.

'I am the boatman' he whispers. 'I am the Magic which steers the boat.' And, pointing again over your shoulder with his uas wand, he adds 'The Nile rises. Light comes...'

Enter the harbour and approach the Henu Boat, its wings folded, its frame bare and untested. Kha'm-uast takes the rudders, you the prow. There is a rising line of pure light beyond the harbour mouth, the Inundation approaches. The wings of the boat flutter open, rainbow and alive, furling back to form the hull. On the harbour walls at either side the shaman-wraiths pace into their places, watching you.

The Nile rises and with it the Light, surging into the harbour. The Henu Boat rises with it, straining against its chains.

'Where?' you ask Kha'm-uast.

But there is really only one place to visit in the first stage of your first Journey up the Nile. Silently, using his uas wand again, Kha'm-uast fastens the Nome Standard for Heliopolis between those weather-beaten towers.

Tense, expectant, you hear the chains of the boat creaking like gulls.

'Aunu' says Kha'm-uast, and with the uttering of the Word the chains snap, the Henu Boat finds its level and you soar against the current, into the symbol and between the gates, out into the Nile...

Whatever you glimpse beyond the symbol should be written down afterward. Whatever you feel or sense should likewise be noted in a special diary.

At the end of every section, or exercise, you should also make a deliberate attempt to 'close down' those psychic senses which will have been stimulated to greater or lesser degrees. You should use whatever technique seems most appropriate: seeing the Nile retreat, fastening the Boat upon its sledge again, walking back across the causeway in a return to the mundane world. Or else you can imagine a great door slamming shut upon your brow, and bolts being thrown; or the head encasing itself in lead swathes, or a simple countdown to zero followed by a stamp of the foot.

Everyone develops their own methods of closing down. Everyone who has got this far with the potential for an actual Journey, will already have some notions.

Even if there is no intention of actively attempting these exercises, or no obvious result having done so, then the merest spark of interest on the reader's part will ensure that even a surface reading of the following chapter on Heliopolis will take on board more than mere words. That spark, and the magical impulse behind this book, will cause unconscious resonance between the spirit of Heliopolis and the psyche of the reader. In its own way, in its own time, Heliopolis will make itself felt in the most surprising ways.

THE CITY OF THE SUN

Aunu is the name given to the capital city of the 13th Nome of Lower Egypt. Variations of the name can read as Annu, Ounu, Iunnu, or even On, as it is described in the Bible.

The hieroglyph for Aunu is:

This may mean 'the Pillared City'. The Greeks, in their usual cavalier fashion, called it something entirely different: they called it Heliopolis, the City of the Sun.

The name Aunu was understood by the Egyptians to extend beyond the city itself, northwards into the region of Bubastis, which in Old Kingdom times was regarded as the eastern sector of the 13th Nome. The Nome itself held the title 'Inviolate Sceptre' which was not without prophecy.

Nothing today remains of Aunu except a single standing obelisk of King Senusert I, from the Middle Kingdom, plus a few scattered and inscribed blocks dating from New Kingdom and Late Period times. Save for that obelisk (a solitary pillar and inviolate sceptre indeed) all else has vanished to the 20th-century eye. Yet at one time, in Kha'm-uast's day, there was nowhere quite like it in the world. So influential was its theological and scholarly outpourings that mighty Karnak was known as the Southern Aunu in a kind of reflected glory.

Physically, at the height of its prestige, Aunu was surrounded by massive brick-built walls which rose to 30 feet in height. The area enclosed by these walls was 3000 by 1500 feet, and 4500 by 3100 feet.

Within these walls were the major temples in a constant process of usage, of building and re-building. When temples ran down, like batteries, new ones were built in their place. The names of the major ones have survived in ancient texts: Mansion of the

Benben, House of the Phoenix, House of the Lapwing, Mansion of the Souls of Aunu, House of the Maid of Aunu, Lower Mansion, Mansion of the Double Lions, plus the House of the North and South which represented the prehistoric shrines of Lower and Upper Egypt.

These latter two shrines were preceded by a court; each House was fronted by columns having either the lily of the South or the papyrus of the North capitals. Within each House was a doorway in the south wall which led, via a winding passage, into a cruciform sanctuary which contained statues of the appropriate Neters, set in niches in the walls.

Not all of these shrines were located in Aunu itself. The beautifully named House of the Lapwing, which had aspects of an Osirian Opet, or 'harem', was situated at Kher-aha, a district to the south of the city. Only certain men were allowed in that shrine, and only at certain times.

Aunu also had special shrines to holy trees. The first of these was the Ishedt Tree in the House of the Phoenix. The Ishedt was a deciduous, fruit bearing tree which Ra was said to have split after defeating his enemies each morning. This was a way of describing the horizon and the sunrise (hence the phoenix). The Ishedt was considered a 'tree of life' upon the leaves of which Thoth and Seshat wrote out the years of life accorded to the king.

There is an echo of this to be found in those folk-tales of trees, shrubs or flowers which wither and die at the same time as their owners. In the pure Egyptian sense, it is another example of the Neters - of the tree and the king being one.

The second tree was the Shendet-Acacia Tree, associated with the Goddess Iusaas who was the tutelary deity of the city. This tree was said to be located on the Primeval Mound, north of the Temple of Ra. The gods were said to have been born under this tree; one of the Pyramid Texts (no. 436) says Horus emerged from the acacia.

The third tree was the Baket-Moringa Tree which had a Mansion named after it. This tree was supposed to be located not far from the Sacred Lake and a 'Circle of Libation' where offerings were made.

Finally, there was a chapel to Atum of the Sycamore Tree. The sycamore had special connotations for the Egyptians, and was either associated with particular neters or given as a neter itself. The 109th chapter of the Book of the Dead mentions 'twin sycamores of turquoise' which stood at the eastern gate of Heaven, the gate out of which Ra emerged each morning. Pyramid Text 916 tells of 'yonder tall sycamore in the east of the sky, quivering of leaves on which the gods sit'. The tree was also a manifestation of Nuit who, in this form, defended Osiris and 'rejuvenated his soul among its branches'.

The names of these gods and goddesses may mean nothing at the moment, but they will start to come alive within our understanding.

Aunu was also associated with certain sacred lakes. The Circle of Libation (Sn kbht) we have already mentioned, and also the smaller Pool of Libation (S kbhw). It was also connected with the Cavern in Per-Hapy (the House of Hapy) to the south-west, where the city's harbour district was found. At certain times, the Osirian Mysteries were enacted at Aunu. The public part of this sacred drama entailed a procession which led from the city southward to Kher-aha, and on to Per-Hapy. This procession was timed to coincide with the yearly rising of the Nile, and the young men of the city vied with one another for the honour of carrying the sacred barque. The image of Osiris was taken out of its shrine (which was uniformly described as magnificent) and carried out of the city on the road to Kher-aha. Once there, Osiris was transferred from one barque to another and taken to Per-Hapy. In the Cavern at Per-Hapy the priests invoked Osiris to release the Nile waters and inundate the fields of Lower Egypt. Timed to perfection (for no true priest is entirely without a little showmanship), water was seen to rush out of the sacred Cavern, and was taken as a signal for general rejoicing. The Inundation was on its way.

Aunu was the place where kings purified themselves. The inundation of the North was said to issue from its territory, just as the Southern inundation was said to issue from Biggah. The health and welfare of the individual and also the nation was dependent upon the regular flow of the sacred waters, and thus the life-giving currents. It was also the place where Hathor was worshipped, and Maat (who is crucial to the 20th and 21st centuries) as well as the Mnevis Bull, the Benben Stone and the Benu Bird. Each of these had either a shrine within the main temples as guest deities, or else temples of their own within the city. And there was also Iusaas herself, the city's own especial deity, whom we shall come to understand when we weave together those strands of light known as the Heliopolitan Rescenscion. Each of these deities or symbols has a resonance within the modern psyche. Each of them has an exquisite though too long forgotten relevance for the modern world. Aunu is alive within us. Although to get there properly we have to consider the dead first.

★

When the dead return to our inner senses they do so in the forms of their greatest vigour. If they do not, then they have clearly not learned much by dying. Only very rarely, except in times of illness or depression, does an eighty year old, for example, feel his age. Throughout their lives people tend to 'stick' inwardly, at a certain age. When they return to us after death they invariably assume the idealised form from their own best years.

As with individuals, no less cities, no less Aunu itself. With a history encompassing thousands of years and countless changes, we can best approach Aunu in its idealised form.

Yet when we enter these places in a magical way we rarely catch any sense of them as architecturally whole - any more than an exiled Parisian would remember his city as a complete unit, with all of the boundaries clearly defined, all of the Quartiers and land-marks proud within his vision. Each person approaching Aunu will catch glimpses: often frozen scenes, or bits and pieces of vision, or remembrance like mirror-shards.

One of the curiosities about Aunu is that each scene contains its own radiance, as though lit from within. This is a sign of Aunu being alive within the psyche - the strange, gentle, and almost smug radiance of an inner sun. Heliopolis/Aunu no longer exists upon the earth, but the City of Sun's power is withdrawn and shining yet, from inward levels.

★

How we approach Aunu from the Henu Boat is a matter for personal experience. Sometimes the vessel fades away, dissolving back into the dream-stuff, and the traveller finds himself within the city. Often it is best to visualise the Henu Boat as coming down and landing outside the city walls, before the gate. In this respect it is interesting to note the number of sacred places in Egypt which actually had replica solar barques outside the walls or ceremonial boat-pits for obscure purposes. We can visualise the Henu Boat, the inner essence of the solar barque, as coming down and blending into these sacred places.

In the latter case, having ' landed' outside the gates we must see them in whatever form they present themselves, but inscribed with the symbol:

which is the hieroglyphic key to the city itself, as opposed to the Nome.

Behind these gates were the inner walls of the city, running parallel and not quite as high, with the rear and often shabby entrances of numerous temples backed onto this space between - their splendours reserved for the inside. Here, in this area between the outer and inner walls, in the shade, were market vendors and tradesfolk of all nationalities, and old priests who were wearied with their divinity taking gentle exercise by walking, sunwise, around the entire complex twice after a heavy lunch.

Often then the Traveller attempts these exercises, in each case trying to retain a sense of Kha'm-uast with him, scenes like the above may flash in upon his consciousness. There may well be a multitude of images, little dramas that enact themselves and which may or may not have reincarnatory import. Often the people in these dramas or rituals, will give off the sense of being intensely aware of *you* - for in a very real sense you will actually be there. Sometimes, however, nothing may seem to happen at all, in any immediate sense; but give it time and Aunu will come through in its own peculiar way.

Whether this is via some gate in time, or through the blessing of an alternative reality is scarcely important. Whether the actual image of Aunu's outer gate is architecturally accurate is also less important than the upwelling of energy from the subconscious which helps to create it. It is not easy to sustain such experiences at the best of times, and by the most experienced of Travellers; so when they happen you must watch, listen, and be modest.

These are all qualities becoming to the visitor.

★

If our notional and exiled Parisian were to have one supreme architectural image reigning above all others when remembering his city, then it would very likely be the Eiffel Tower. If we, as notional and exiled citizens of Aunu were to have similar, it would certainly be that of the Benben column. In this first visit to Aunu, making our way through the outer and inner gates of the double walls, across the great courtyard through the throng of people, we stand at the northern side of the square where the tip of its noon-day shadow almost touched our feet.

The Benben is no more than a monument shaped thus:

In a literal sense it contains the true spirit of Aunu, both as a symbol of its theology, an expression of its powers, and focus for the past and future souls of the place. The nearest modern equivalent (in Britain at least) is the local war-memorial dedicated to those village souls who sacrificed themselves for 'the Supreme Good', and who are said to live on yet through the inscriptions, aided by annual ceremonies involving wreaths of poppies. Likewise, in pre-historic Britain, the crude but none the less potent standing-stones were first cousins to the Benben.

The Benben was unique to Aunu, and reflected the antiquity of the city's solar worship. It was the forerunner, or prototype of the obelisk, but was a shorter and more squat version of those tall and grandiose obelisks which graced the front of temples. It was made of white stone, pure white stone surmounted by a golden pyramidion which dazzled when the sun shone upon it.

See it now with Kha'm-uast behind you, his uas wand upon your temple, and behind him the open, imposing, glowing columns of the House of the Phoenix. See the light spurting from the pillar's top as Earth mates with Sky, and divisions are resolved. See the shadow of the Benben cast upon the ground and the splume of light from the pyramidion playing around its tip, so that we can actually see a reflection of the dark member of the Earth God entering the radiant sex of the Sky Goddess. Feel beneath your toes the deeply enscribed flag-stones of the courtyard on which the cycles of man, the world and the universe are given, which serve a calendrical purpose at very least, and which young children with stiff brooms regularly sweep clean. Then hear Kha'm-uast's voice while he tells the story of those deities which we know today as the Heliopolitan Rescenscion.

Aunu may have disappeared from the face of the earth, but its *ka* lives on within these tales...

★

In the beginning there was nothingness, and darkness, and ever-lasting night, without beginning and without end. This was the realm of Nun, which we might mispronounce as None and get some idea of the emptiness involved.

Into this realm came the god Atum - a statement which can be revised and extended by saying: the god Atum came into this realm, and manifestation began.

Atum, as sniggering Egyptian children knew, masturbated the universe into existence.

This was the primordial sexual act: Atum, known as 'the

Great He/She', mating with himself and producing the universe from his seed. Or, to give it a feminist gloss, Atum, mating with herself and producing the universe from her climax. Either interpretation is valid. The crux of the matter is that once, in the heart of darkness, Atum came, and life began.

One way or another, it is a revelation that we have all known.

As far as cosmologies go it is also very close to that of the Hebrew Qabalah in which Chockmah, or God-becoming-aware-of-himself, awakens from the 'Nun-like' realm of Ain Soph, sees that he exists, and gives out that first shout of laughter and surprise which we would think of now as the Big Bang. Given that Chockmah's esoteric symbols include the phallus, the rod and the standing stone, we might assume that the priests of Israel learned a great deal more than how to make bricks during their enforced sojourn in On, as they called it.

Spurting semen, climaxes, laughter and Big Bangs - they are modern vulgarities of interpretation and word-play but yet intensely valid to the way that such things were once seen and understood in Aunu, which was regarded as the actual place where the god 'came' to earth.

As time went on, however, and the concepts generally became more personalised, Atum became more of a man and less an abstract principle. So his hand, with which he masturbated, became his consort. This 'hand-goddess', the butt of many delightfully wicked jokes, was called Iusaas, or 'She who comes is mighty'. She had her own special shrine in Aunu. In a sense she was Aunu itself.

This is indicated by the hieroglyph for the city which can be broken down as follows:

nu - town, or city

nu - liquid

an - given as 'pillar', or 'light tower(?)' as Budge rather hesitatingly puts it, but which is a stumble toward the Benben's function.

In one translation Aunu/Annu is the 'City of the Shining Pillar of Liquid', which is a clear enough reference to the Benben being regarded as a solidified column of Atum's semen.

In another sense, looking into the symbolism a little more deeply, it becomes the 'City which is the Container (∪) of the Shining Pillar' - an allusive reference to the hand which contains the penis.

Iusaas, then, is self-knowledge (corrupted by Victorians into 'self-abuse') - or personal gnosis. It is the simplest and most fundamental of all revelations.

★

But not all of the Creation tales placed such an emphasis upon masturbation - only the popular ones. The Shu Texts evoke an image of a perch extending from the Abyss, from the heart of Nun, on which is perched that grey heron known as the Benu Bird 'Who determines what is, and what is not to be'. When it opens its beak it utters what is essentially the Word, a call to life and cyclicity across the silence of the ancient night. Esoterically this heron became the 'soul' of Osiris in some analyses, and symbol for the planet Venus - that morning star which precedes the sun out of the Underworld. It is the harbinger of good tidings, the herald of new dispensations, and perhaps the most august link between this realm and the 'Isle of Fire' - a magical place of eternal light where gods are born and revived, and from which they are sent out into the world.

In crude terms every time we climax we utter the cry of the Benu Bird, the heron; and so on more levels than one Aunu is the place in Ancient Egypt from which all comes.

★

Atum, who later became known as Atum-Re, was symbolised by:

which is a reference to the Primordial Mound - another of his titles. The mound in question is the First Matter in the abstract sense, and an actual geographical location within the boundaries of Aunu where the gods came to earth and conjoined the worlds. Another symbol which relates to the same impulse is that of the Benu Bird upon its perch - again a pyramidal mound:

In Utterance 600 of the Pyramid Texts, yet another version is given. Instead of the next phase of creation (Atum's two children) being born from his seed, they are instead spat out of his mouth - 'You spat forth as Shu, you expectorated as Tefnut, you put your arms around them in an act of Ka-giving so that your Ka might be in them.'

Shu's name is derived from a verb which means 'to raise'. It can be translated as 'he who holds up'. As emptiness deified he became a god of air in an abstract sort of way, for no especial cult grew up around him. Like oxygen, he was seen as being everywhere within the dome of the world, supporting all life, yet not exactly the most visible of gods.

Created by the same semen/spit/heron-cry was his twin sister Tefnut, who was likewise seen more as a theological concept, a goddess of moisture to moderate and give vitality to the otherwise arid qualities of Shu. Tefnut, however, very quickly became identified with the goddess Maat, who has suffered a little by being translated as Truth, Justice or World Order. In fact she is more accurately known as the Balance of Nature, which is what the rather old-fashioned concept of World Order was stumbling toward. Maat is ergonomic, eco-friendly, fuel efficient, recyclable. She is the food chain, the rain forest and the ozone layer; she is the magical currents within the psyche and the hormones in the blood. Her symbol is a feather. Shu makes love to her by blowing on her. The rippling of a feather is the love-dance of Maat. Maat is the most delicate of deities. She is also the most powerful.

In the world-pictures of Egyptian art we are shown Shu and Tefnut in a mid-position between their children, Nuit and Geb (of whom more presently) doing that which is necessary to maintain certain natural harmonies. In an elemental sense this is the interaction of Air (Shu), Water (Tefnut), Earth (Geb), and Fire (Nuit). If they do not interact as they do, the heavens will be sterile, the earth will not plant its seed.

Whatever god or goddess may be ruling the aeon it is Maat who always rules behind the scenes. She maintains the balance.

★

From them were born two children: Geb, who inherited Shu's crown and became known as the Earth God, and Nu (also called Nuit, or Nut) who was the goddess of the heavenly vaults, the stars. Those 'fires' with which she equates are the stellar fires. Shu is the atmosphere, but Nu is beyond that as the vault of the stars. She is shown as a beautiful, gracefully arched woman who is forever poised above her brother and lover, Geb. Only at night can the stars come down to earth and they can mate. Every morning at dawn Shu and Tefnut separate them again.

The magical lesson involved here is that the stars and the earth belong to each other. They should be locked in an eternal embrace, an ever-coming cosmic fusion, but in order to allow life to enter into such a relationship Shu and Tefnut must become involved in momentary separations, so that the world can be born between them. The only thing that sustains them is the knowledge that at night Shu and Tefnut will also guide them back onto each other again. We on earth need the stellar divinities and conscious-ness. Those 'beyond the stars' also need us here on earth.

★

Geb is that erotic, sensual feeling that the earth in its splendour can often evoke within us. The sense (not clearly defined but very strong) that if we could only unite with the spirit of the land beneath then we might in some way touch the stars.

Nu is the power of Womanhood - dark and glittering and infinite who knows the secret of keeping Man prone, erect, and forever striving to reach her. Nu has the sort of power which modern women (Nu/New Women) are re-learning.

★

It is in considering the four children of Nu and Geb that we find ourselves approaching the very heart of the Aunu mysteries. Their children were known as Osiris, Isis, Nephthys and Set; their basic story is simple enough.

Osiris and Isis, who are more properly called Asar and Aset, fell in love within the womb. Set and Nephthys, in contrast, had no such happy relationship. Osiris and Isis, who might be regarded as the Golden Couple, were so loving, and so loved, so full of grace and fortune, that Set was always going to hate them. This hate was intensified for two reasons: First, Osiris had been given the Earth God's crown when Geb had tired of its weight, and Set had long coveted this for himself; second, Nephthys so loved her brother Osiris that she used a magical, shape-shifting ruse to sleep with him, which resulted in her bearing his child.

In time Set slew Osiris and cut his body into 14 pieces, and scattered them throughout Khem.

In her despair Isis travelled throughout the land and, with the help of Nephthys' child Anubis, eventually found and re-assembled the pieces, all saving the phallus which had been swal-lowed by a fish. Undaunted she created a golden phallus for him, and with her own magical arts vitalised this enough to make herself pregnant by a lover who was still, essentially, in the Underworld.

At this point, although Osiris had the choice of returning to the world of men instead of continuing to exist within the Duat, he chose to remain where he was, in what is almost a reversal of the Christian resurrection. Osiris chose to go 'down', while Jesus opted for the 'up'.

Isis, by now heavily pregnant and in great danger from Set, made her way to the Isle of Khebit where she gave birth to Horus, the Hawk God. Between them, she and Nephthys taught the initially sickly wonderchild all those fighting arts which would enable him finally to wrest the Earth God's crown from his usurper uncle.

In time, after years of combat, he did exactly that.

This is a simple precis of the most basic version of the tale but it will do for now. It is not always wise to clutter the Henu Boat with too much cargo.

★

Osiris was depicted in two forms, often conjoined: as a Green Man quite literally - who naturally represented the fertility of the earth forces and the similar qualities among the people; and also as a Horned God, as shown by the *atef* crown which was a tribute to his own generative powers (more dead than alive, he *still* managed to get his wife pregnant). In either or both of his roles the common people made corn dollies in tribute; they had what we might think of as Harvest Festivals. As with all those Horned Gods who once claimed the loyalties of pre-historic and even Medieval Europeans, Osiris was essentially the god of the common folk in the early days. His phallus, swallowed by the fish of the Piscean Age, will be found when Aquarian man empties his pitcher and reveals that same fish flapping its last at the bottom. Gut the fish and Man will have a chance of being whole again.

★

Isis likewise has become universalised as her own early followers increased in numbers and passion at a rate which almost left the Aunu priesthood unprepared. Isis' hieroglyph is that of a seat, a throne, symbol of the stability that she gives to any situation, as well as that maternal quality of taking small, helpless souls into her presence, seating them down and making them feel kinglike.

She is also that sense within us, during our formative years, which tells us that no matter how stupid we are, no matter how cruel or inept or ineffective in all other areas of life, that our mother loves us no matter what. In fact 'No matter what...' might almost be her motto as far as some individuals and societies are concerned. If we have Isis within us then *no matter what*, we can endure.

★

Nephthys is different. Her symbol is that of a chalice. She accepts whatever we put into it. She will become whatever we want her to become. When we see liquid adapting to the shape of the vessel, that is Nephthys.

It is not so much that she sits down and endures, but that she takes on forms to survive. Nephthys was the original Single Parent, who became so by choice. She is to be found when women enter professions which were hitherto the exclusive reserve of the male. She is glimpsed in those women who choose to be mistress, rather than wife. There are some obvious areas of overlap with Isis, of course, but they did share a womb together after all.

★

Set, of course, attracts the scorn and the venom, and yet it is his darkness which makes the other shine. Without him to show us what darkness means, we could never appreciate the qualities of light and goodness emanated by the other three.

Set, who is also Shaitan or Satan, is still the true lord of this world at present. Horus has not yet challenged him; Osiris has not

yet found his true potency within the Underworld, or the Duat. We encounter Set during those times in life when we feel torn apart, and scattered. Yet by learning to rebuild ourselves, and discover new potentials for fertility, we can make Set become the most potent initiator of all.

★

Horus, like his great grandfather Shu, is 'that which rises up', as opposed to 'raises up'. Traditionally described as being crippled at birth, or deformed below the waist (an echo of his neutered father, perhaps) his own power is found within his arms: they are wings; he soars.

Horus, or Heru to give him his proper name, is *the* wonderchild, the spirit of the next Aeon. When the Aquarian pitcher spills out its fish it will be Horus who will swoop down and rip it open. Once that lost part is reclaimed mankind will begin to make steps that will take humanity home again, back to wholeness, back to the source.

Horus (and Anubis) are figures of extreme importance in the present Journey. They are templates against which all the rest can be compared. The danger of the Heliopolitan Rescenscion is that the student can find it hard to break away. Iusaas/Aunu take on siren-like qualities which can pull the unwary traveller not onto rocks, but into the ivory tower of the academic - which in itself is the poor man's alternative to the Benben.

We will come back to the deities of Aunu later, in our own time, when we have substance enough as Travellers to be able to cope with them.

★

Like the spurting of a fountain, or the climax of Atum (whose solidified column of semen is represented by the Benben) these deeds and misdeeds among the gods are *always happening*. This is what the Qabalists would refer to as 'Eheieh asher Eheieh' in describing their own Source, meaning 'I am the Ever-becoming One'.

They are not events (mythical/historical or otherwise) which occur in linear time, with clearly defined beginnings and endings; they are happening within us now, if we know how to look. The Benben column that we should now start to visualise again, can be as relevant to ourselves as it was during the millenia of Aunu's splendour.

Turn around and in your mind's eye see Kha'm-uast standing before the huge but reed-like pillars of the House of the Phoenix. He is dressed now as the High Priest of Aunu, a role which as Royal Heir he was fully entitled to assume, much as the British monarch is regarded as the head of the Church of England, and of all the military forces too.

In highly esoteric terms (which can be ignored if the Traveller so wishes) Aunu is linked with what the Qabalists would term the Sphere of Daath, or Knowledge. Again this does not refer to knowledge in the academic sense (which is ultimately a very inferior kind of understanding) but with that intensity of revelation which comes from personal experience, crudely but adequately depicted in the old sense of a man *knowing* a woman. In the micro-cosmic man Daath is linked with that 'sacred centre' known within the eastern tradition as the Visuddhi Chakra, which is the spiritualised aspect of the thyroid gland. In this scheme the sphere of Daath also takes in the functions of the pituitary gland (and Alexandria later took on Aunu's role as the centre of learning, becoming the home of the Gnostics) as well as the pineal gland (and it was on Khebit that Horus, whose symbol is an eye, was born).

Even more esoterically Daath was the sphere, or realm,

occupied by humanity before the Fall into Matter. Daath represents those realms of pure gnosis in which mankind existed before plummeting down through the worlds and into manifestation, into life on Earth.

Aunu at the throat-centre is life giving voice to itself. Daath is the Hidden Sphere, represented on the Tree of Life by just a circle of dots and the most elusive of imagery. Aunu/Heliopolis today consists of only a few stones.

★

All this and more is passed across by Kha'm-uast in the most subtle of ways. There are also more than a few hints of it to be found in the stole he wears as High Priest of Aunu.

To the Ancient Egyptians, the symbol ✕ referred to the heavens above. ⊗ on the other hand, was the symbol for the Duat, or the 'heavens below'. The significance of this, and the foregoing, will become clearer later. A conscious understanding is not necessary at this stage; even as we read this, if there is any spark of interest at all, the Henu Boat of our innermost self will already be making its own voyage toward the truth of it all.

In essence we can reach the stars by sending our consciousness up into the skies, or down below the earth. There is not a great deal of difference.

★

Although Aunu was best known as the City of the Sun it honoured the moon and stars also. Aunu was called 'the horizon of the sky' as well as 'the sky of Egypt'. Lunar festivals took place there at the new moon, the 6th day of the month, full moon and last quarter, while special attention was paid to the starry night sky, and regular ceremonies devoted to the Mysteries of Nu taking place in the chamber called the 'Star Room' in the Temple of Ra.

One of the magical symbols of the city was that ✕ shown upon Kha'm-uast's stole, usually depicted on temple reliefs as mounted on a standard carried by priests - an origin, perhaps, of the fairy wand that has become so trivialised. The High Priest of Aunu was known as the 'Greatest of Seers'; he was the chief astronomer/astrologer for the whole country. Other titles he bore included: 'He who discloses the secrets of Heaven', 'Supervisor of the Mysteries of Heaven' - both of which were further expanded as 'He who perceives the Mysterious One of Heaven' and 'Master of the Mystery of the Secrets of Heaven'. Yet further titles included 'Imy-is' which means 'He who is in the chapel of Shu and Tefnut' and also (more poignantly) 'Nb-wny', which means 'Lord of Light'.

★

See him now, before that House of the Phoenix which can give us renewal if we so need it, see him now the Lord of Light with his uas wand touching your throat, the brilliance which had begun in your pituitary, carried inward to your pineal, and brought down now into the thyroid.

★

Playing the Game of the Neters again, we must note how this gland consists of two lateral lobes, conical in shape, connected by an isthmus which passes transversely across the trachea. A third lobe called the pyramid sometimes arises from the upper part of the isthmus or from one of the lobes, generally on the left side. Occasionally the lobe is found to be detached.

The function of this gland is to produce the hormone thyroxin, which increases the rate of metabolism. In amphibia, it is thyroxin which causes metamorphosis: tadpoles change into frogs, or 𓆣 change into 𓃒 .

If Aunu is one lobe of this gland then the other lobe is to be found across the River Nile, on the Giza plateau. There, approached via a lion which is changing into a man from the head down, lies one centre of metamorphosis that no-one can ignore.

★

Tombs were always important in the ancient world. Tombs and wombs were regarded as different aspects of the same thing, giving a soul birth into worlds. To the pharaonic mind the tomb was a thing for eternity, while their actual palaces were built of the same mudbrick as the commoner, as testament to the ephemeral nature of their lives. The forces which governed life upon the earth would focus upon the proper functioning of the womb; the forces which governed life in the Otherworld would direct themselves toward the tomb.

The earliest royal tombs of the 1st and 2nd Dynasties were of the type now known as 'mastaba', from an Arabic word meaning 'bench', suggestive of the overall shape and appearance of the tombs. They were low, rectangular structures consisting of a substructure, the burial pit, and the mastaba-shaped superstructure built over it. The similarity between these and the early chambered tombs of Europe has often been remarked upon. The mastaba tombs of the early kings and queens could be large, many-chambered structures often built to resemble their earthly dwelling places: that which was best about their temporal life was not going to be jettisoned in the spiritual. The similarity was also another way of helping both parties (living and deceased) to maintain contact. Losing contact between the worlds was a thing of dread to the Ancient Egyptian.

The low mastaba tombs were symbolic of the Primeval Hill, the first firmament to rise out of the watery chaos of Nun at the beginning of time and creation. In this symbolic sense the mastaba tombs were their owners hopes of a spiritual rebirth. It was the mighty Imhotep, architect to King Djoser, who took this concept a step further with his creation of the famous Step Pyramid complex at Saqqara.

Upon the Primeval Hill at its first rising was the self-created Sun God, Atum-Ra. As we have seen the priests of Aunu had developed the shape of the Primeval Hill into the Benben, that squat obelisk with its golden pyramidion tip representing the presence of the Sun God. Imhotep, familiar with this image from Aunu where he had served as High Priest in his time, incorporated this shape and its solar iconography into his design for Djoser's tomb. In effect he placed Primeval Hills one upon the other, each succeeding one smaller than the one beneath, first four high and then six, to form the steps. Djoser was to be able to figuratively and symbolically climb his own stairway to heaven using the architectural innovation of this structure. From the Sun Priest's point of view Imhotep built his massive Benben at Saqqara so that the soul of his king might climb the steps up to the top and alight from it as a Benu, or spiritual winged soul.

In a real sense there are some magical mechanics - spiritual aerodynamics - involved here. We can glimpse them in the old western tradition which says that certain places - invariably hilltops - become gathering places for the souls of the dead. At certain times these souls are gathered up from such way-stations and taken onward, into the Otherworld.

The earliest pyramid was to do much the same thing - not only for Djoser himself, but for all of his people too.

But Imhotep built more than just a tomb for Djoser: he included a virtual palace city, complete with everything that the king would need in the future life. The royal needs included space for the burial of his family, a replica of his palace, an entire Heb-Sed court, enough chapels to include each of the important neters, shrines to represent the two halves of the country, and great open courts where the souls of the dead could stroll beneath an everlasting light. The entire complex was over a mile in length and completely surrounded by massive walls 33 feet high. Yet it was the pyramidal shape of the tomb itself that made the most impression upon later kings and architects - not only through the dynasties of historical Egypt, but throughout the world and up until our present time also. It was this shape that was employed to carry the design a step further to evolve into the true pyramid of the 4th Dynasty. (See Figure 8.)

In a sense (perhaps more senses than one) the pyramids were like the nuclear reactors of today, both in terms of the technological achievement and the sheer labour involved. Like nuclear reactors they can also be immensely dangerous: we can fall into them, and/ or have them blow up in our faces if we don't have adequate psychological damping rods.

For centuries now they have been the focus of every esoteric idiosyncrasy. Freemasons, Rosicrucians, Theosophists, Ufologists and every kind of seer and prophet has used them within their own revelations - quite apart from those 'Pyramid Inchers' who insist that the future of the world up until the Second Coming and beyond is clearly defined within the mathematical proportions.

In another sense the pyramid is the masculine counterpart to the Holy Grail - that mystic cup which brought both revelation and salvation. In contrast to the Grail's passive and receptive qualities the pyramid would hold, channel, and direct our inner potentials in much the same way as the phallus does the sperm.

The wonders connected with the Great Pyramid of Khufu are frequently listed and easily summarised:

The proportions of the Great Pyramid contain a precise knowledge of the Earth's circumference, including its flattening at the poles. They demonstrate exactly the number π, and the four sides are aligned to the cardinal points of the compass with an accuracy to within 1/12 of a degree - and even this error may well have been due to to a shifting of the Earth's axis. Acting as a sundial its shadow to the North annually marked the solstices and equinoxes, and gave the Egyptian priests an unrivalled knowledge of the sun and earth's relationship. Many of the stones, some almost 70 tons, were so exquisitely cut and placed that the joints between them were less than 1/50th inch in thickness. And given the disputed time-scale for the construction, they were either laid at an unbelievable rate over many generations, or an impossible rate over a few. Once laid (and no-one is entirely certain how this was done) they were given an outer casing of polished limestone which was honed to the standards of modern optical work.

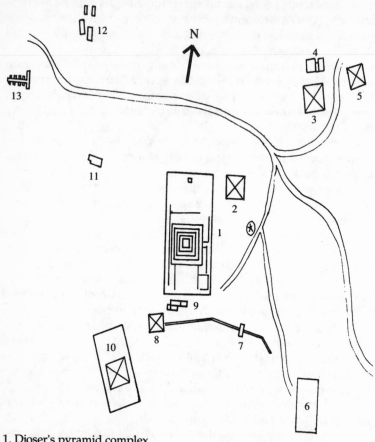

1. Djoser's pyramid complex.
2. Userkaf's complex.
3. Teti's pyramid.
4. Tombs of Mereruka, Kagemni, Ankh-mahor.
5. Ruined pyramid, unidentified.
6. Valley Temple of Unas.
7. Tombs of Khnum-hotep and Ni-ankh-Khnum.
8. Pyramid of Unas.
9. Tomb of Idut.
10. Pyramid complex of Sekhemkhet.
11. Tomb of Ptah-hotep.
12. Tomb of Ti.
13. Serapeum - Tomb of Kha'm-uast.

Figure 8 - Imhotep's burial complex built for Djoser at Saqqara

Two major divergences of opinion are as to whether the Great Pyramid was ever used as a tomb, or was instead a centre for initiation. Convincing arguments can be marshalled for and against both,

While in the present scheme we are suggesting that they form one of the lateral lobes in the spiritual equivalent of Inner Egypt's thyroid gland, creating and regulating magical energies which are directly equivalent to those hormones secreted by our own, physical glands, influencing reproduction, growth, differentiation and metabolism; as well as activating the migratory impulses in salmon - a fish regarded in western mythology as the purest expression of Knowledge.

In short there is room within any pyramid for all of mankind's idiosyncrasies. These are what help us grow. Idiosyncrasy can take us far closer to the spirit of Aunu and its 'I am that I am' undertones than mere dogma. In fact dogma is what occurs when idiosyncrasy becomes calcified: our skeletons fail to develop, or else become cranky. We approach pyramids in a cloud of unknowing and will eventually leave them with Revelation - which proves that they are wondrously effective agents for transmutation if we can only approach them in the right sense, with the peculiar lightness of spirit that Kha'm-uast himself radiated.

★

Just as the influential priesthood of Aunu had provided the guidelines for the early mastaba tombs and step pyramids, they now provided the impetus for these huge pyramids of the 4th Dynasty, for the High Priest of Aunu was a Lord of Light in the same sense that the senior officer in the British Navy is known as the First Sea Lord. Light was the medium with which he was concerned - quite literally, in its reflective sense.

If Aunu itself represented life giving voice to itself, then the pyramids across the river were words frozen in stone, for the future.

The hieroglyph for pyramid was, not surprisingly $\triangle$. The fact that the symbol for Sothis, or Sirius, was $\triangle$ shows that among the most infinite range of pyramidal symbolism was another of these references to mankind's relationship with certain stars. $\triangle$ represents Sothis on earth.

The architectural change from the stepped pyramid to the true pyramids on the Giza plateau reflected the Aunu priesthood's own shift from a stellar orientation to one that was fully solar. This can be seen in the fact that the accompanying mortuary temples of the step pyramids were situated toward the north, the direction of the circumpolar stars. This was in accordance with the sacred texts which required that the dead king be provided with a stairway to the undying stars: '...a stairway to the sky is set up for you among the Imperishable Stars'. Imhotep had done just this for Djoser, but with the application of the glass-smooth casings of white limestone, different techniques were brought into play. On the pyramids of Giza the very rays of the sun were now to be the medium by which dead souls would reach heaven. Instead of stepping up to the stars the idea was that the king's soul would ascend on the light of the sun itself. The stellar stairways of Imhotep became a thing of the past. Everything hinged upon solar power in this new age that the Aunu priesthood entered.

This period also saw a change in religious ideology which increasingly focussed upon the burgeoning cult of Osiris, causing the attendant mortuary temples to be oriented toward the East, now, and the rising sun. It is as though the priesthood stopped looking backward to a possible origin among the circumpolar stars and started looking forward.

So esoterically each stage from early mastaba to true pyramid represents an evolving religious concept: 1. the Primeval Hill, 2. a stairway to the stars, 3. the sun's rays captured in stone. Each stage was successively higher - in both literal and figurative terms - than the preceding one, and the common factor was an expression in physical terms of the soul's symbolic ascent back to heaven.

Here, in an architectural sense, was matter diminishing toward spirit; while at another level here was Geb (the Earth) mating with Nu (the Sky) in what might be regarded as the ultimate expression of the material and spiritual worlds in perfect union.

★

We can visit the Pyramids with Kha'm-uast. The precise details of how we get there must be left to the individual imagination. If he or she does not possess this, then they will not get far upon the Journey.

In crossing the Nile toward Giza we are in effect directing our consciousness towards the other lobe of the thyroid gland, as well as the parathyroid. The latter, as the name implies, cannot really be separated from its parent body and usually consists of four glands, one pair below and one pair embedded in the thyroid itself. How these relate to specific sites, items or temples, is a matter for the individual to determine when he plays the Game of the Neters.

The parathyroid glands are involved in the secretion of a hormone which controls the calcium and phosphorus mechanism. Neither of these substances occur in nature in the free state, but usually in the form of phosphates. Various compounds of phosphorus are found in the animal body, such as in the brain and nerves. Calcium phosphate, for example, forms 60% of the substance needed for bones; it is also found in all fertile soils.

The Aunu/Pyramid centres produce energies that are directly equivalent to these substances. The River Nile begins its northern Inundation from Aunu: the magical equivalents of calcium phosphate, which are vital to the Nile Valley's abundant fertility, are also emanated from here. Similarly, we may have fallen into matter as pure spirit, but it is through our bone structure and properly regulated growth mechanisms that we can make the best of our lot and start to manipulate the world of matter.

Calcium is a silver-white metal forming hexagonal crystals. Calcium and phosphorus can also burn in the air with a very intense white light: the same sort of light which will be seen from Aunu, dancing from the Pyramids - the same sort of light which will draw our Henu Boat across the Nile to land between the paws of the Sphinx.

★

The Sphinx, which may well have things of its own to tell you about the nature of divinity trapped within an animal body, knows how the mind can be used to transmute form. Even to the Ancient Egyptians, however, it was never always entirely visible. Every decade or so the hollow in which it stands would fill with sand, so that only the head remained above the desert and the mystery of its dual nature lost to another generation.

Many unorthodox students insist that the Sphinx is the oldest man-made object on this planet, dating back to a time when Egypt was ruled directly by the neters, and then the Shemsu Hor, or Companions of Horus. If anything or anyone knows the truth about the Fall, it does.

Among the many other peculiarities of this peculiar area is the fairly widely accepted belief that it lies upon the exact centre of the land-mass of the northern hemisphere. Were we to strip the continents from the globe and balance them upon a needle-point (a Benben?) then the centre of balance would be at Giza.

The Sphinx, like the pyramids themselves, is something that every Traveller must approach themselves in their own way. But in general terms it is a symbol which is echoed in the Aker, guarding

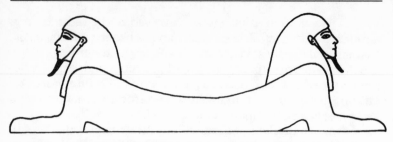

the gates to the Underworld, and thus each Traveller's own subconscious.

The Aker is a sphinx-like creature which was said to guard the eastern and western gates to the Underworld, or the Duat. Basic Egyptian cosmology, of the sort taught to the youngest children, posited Three Worlds:

Spiritual (represented by $\times$)

Material (represented by ▭)

Underworld (represented by $\bigotimes$)

Using this basic grouping, and bearing in the mind the old dictum 'As above, so below', we can parallel them with others:

Spiritual	Divine	Supraconsciousness
Material	Human	Mundane consciousness
Underworld	Animal	Subconsciouness

If the Aker, whose head is in our world and whose body is 'below' (often literally under the sand as with the Great Sphinx), were to hold any symbol between its paws it would be that of the disk $\bigotimes$ which is really more like the closed neck of the cervix. By going via the $\bigotimes$ we can, if we understand our magic, also pick up an understanding of the other two worlds which mirror it.

There has also long been a tradition of a secret tunnel leading from the Sphinx to the Great Pyramid, though we should never put too much stock in that. Secret tunnels are almost *de rigueur* for any place touched by the numinous. Yet although such a tunnel almost certainly does not exist in the material world, there is definitely one which drives through the subconscious, the dream-world, which the Traveller may care to unearth for him/herself.

However we get there, however we enter, the interior of the

Great Pyramid will always be one of enormous familiarity. As we stumble down the Descending Passage which was originally aligned northward to Alpha Draconis at its lower culmination, we can feel ourselves entering denser and denser levels of matter, into that darkness which is only rarely touched by the Dragon Star. The atmosphere can be appalling if the Traveller happens to be there (and he always is) when the star hoves into sight: there is a sense of despair and desolation - of being trapped, weighed down. A sense of unutterable loneliness. A cry in the throat is felt which is the direct opposite of the life-cry given by the Benu Bird at time's dawn; this is the death-rattle of the spirit, the cry of Sokaris which is translated as 'Come to me quickly!', and which is the eternal and cyclical counterpart to the Benu Bird's 'I come!'

It intensifies until we find ourselves in the Subterranean Chamber.

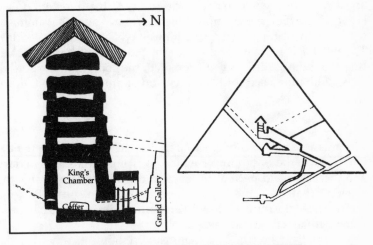

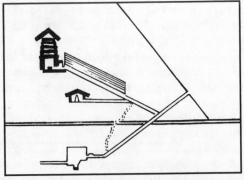

Figure 9 - Inside the Great Pyramid

This, we quickly realise, is a place that we know only too well: after a long, despairing slide then comes the formless, hard place of absolute darkness with a dead-end passage behind us (and how often have we all taken *that* route?), an apparently bottomless pit somewhere off to one side, obstacles all around, and at best - at very best - a long, difficult and cramped climb back up the way we have just tumbled.

No need to travel to Egypt to enter the Great Pyramid. No need to effect a magical entry. One way or another we've all been there many times.

★

So the cry 'Come to me quickly' may be the initiatory cry, but before we can hear the Benu's response we must, in ourselves, have the overwhelming desire to rise to the light. At that   moment does the spirit of Osiris *begin* to awaken within us. At that moment do we *begin* to have the chance of mastering the Duat. And at that moment, too, we may begin to hear Osiris himself whisper 'I am Yesterday, Today, and Tomorrow; and I have the power to be born a second time. I am the hidden soul who createth the gods. I am the Lord of those who are raised up from the dead...I am Osiris, the Lord of Eternity.'

★

The moment that we begin to climb what is now, to our new perspective, the Ascending Passage (which contains a secondary and hitherto unsuspected route up to the other chambers) is the moment that we activate the phosphorus, so to speak. It is the moment that the pure white light and inner light of Osiris begins to shine with its unmistakeable flame.

Finally, when the Traveller visualises himself as lying in the sarcophagus in the King's Chamber, aware of the collossal mass of stone all around him, the meaning of the pyramid will begin to reveal itself.

Concerned as we are with the uniqueness of the individual, it is impossible to say exactly what will be experienced. A dozen different people may have a dozen completely conflicting revelations of varying intensity. They will all be correct, all be true. Sometimes it will be like being a note in a great, low, and very slow song whose notes ripple back and forth across the universe like waves. Other times, the walls of the pyramid will become glass, you will find yourself no longer prone but pushing through space at unimaginable speed, the bulk of the pyramid's base behind you like some engine, the apex of the pyramid crystal clear before you as you rush toward the stars. Or else you may feel that you are in some sense the spiritual equivalent of a sperm cell caught up in some eternal cosmic mating.

Idiosyncrasies will determine the nature of these revelations within the Great Pyramid. They will be right and true within our own universe if no-one else's.

★

We can, and should, visit the other pyramids of the Giza complex as we seek to adjust the endocrine balance of the world at large. Whether we choose to visualise Kha'm-uast as being present throughout is a matter for the individual Traveller, but as a cautionary measure, no-one should visit Snefru's Pyramid without him. The atmosphere there is something different again, not easily coped with. Nor should anyone attempt to visit them all, magically, in a single evening, but spread the explorations over the weeks, entering on impulse. There should be no sense of haste involved. The pyramids won't go away. That, after all, is one of their primary functions.

★

Aunu's influence lasted for almost 2000 years, even though after the Pyramid Age it never quite regained its level of influence or power. Throughout pharaonic times it remained a city renowned for its learning centres and its sages, despite the fact that during the New Kingdom the revenues coming into the main temples were considerably reduced. The lion's share of the country's resources were by this time destined for the other Aunu, the Southern Aunu, Thebes - and the massive temples of Amun, which we shall visit in due course. Later still, during the Ptolemaic and Roman times, the administrative and economic activities of the city were shifted to Kher-aha, which was nearer the harbour of Per-Hapy and hence the busy river traffic, making communication and transportation easier to maintain.

Once Egypt came under Roman rule, and Aunu's diminished revenues were reduced even further, the famed institutions of the city collapsed. Ptolemaic-influenced and Roman-ruled Alexandria eclipsed the glory of pharaonic Aunu. During the Ptolemaic era some of the scholars of Aunu had left for Alexandria 'where their reputation for learning caused them to be welcomed'. Strabo considered himself lucky to see even the largely deserted Heliopolis and what remained of the sun-temple. He reported that some priests were still in the city, living like ghostly shadows and continuing to perform the old ceremonies. With the dawning of Christianity the ancient temples were torn down and used as building material for Coptic monasteries and Byzantine churches. Obelisks, memorial stelae and other, small, portable items were carried off to Alexandria and Rome, and even further afield in modern times. In 1853 the traveller Richard Lepsius made a trip to the ruins of Heliopolis, the Biblical On, whence Joseph took his wife Asnath, the daughter of a priest, and found nothing but Senusert's obelisk remaining. At that time a garden had been made around it which had flowers lush enough to attract a quantity of bees. These, as Lepsius noted, 'could find no more commodious lodging than in the deep and sharply cut hieroglyphics of the obelisk...'

Kha'm-uast would have been pleased at that.

The City of the Sun which once, more than any other in Egypt reflected the heights of heaven and earth, may only survive today via that single, bee-loud column, but the inner light behind it is undimmed.

MEMPHIS

Sometimes, when we go looking for the sources and meaning of life, we have to approach them via the lands of the dead. Often, conditioned as we are by a culture which associates death with finality and despair, we fail to see the ongoing light within. In Khem, if we know where to look and how to listen, we can find places of the dead that ring with laughter and music - the same joys that European peasants once heard when they put their ears to the fairy knolls of their prehistoric forebears.

To get to Hi-Ka-Ptah, in Memphis, we should really approach it via the huge funerary complexes which curve around the western outskirts. Here, at Saqqara, the dead were given more attention than anywhere else in history. By visiting Saqqara we can give Death back some of its dignity.

★

Many place-names in present-day Egypt are derived from Arabic, although the sites in question are sometimes better known by their earlier Greek corruptions of Egyptian originals. At Saqqara, however, we can find Sokaris again in a relatively unsullied form.

We have already seen his head on the top of the Henu Boat, looking so far into the past that we just know that he can see the whole of the future too. We have called upon him in the subterranean chamber of the Great Pyramid. One way or another we all call upon him at the moment of our own deaths, his name echoing down that tunnel which invariably opens before us, the 'Come to me quickly' summoning love and guidance from the Otherworld.

Where there is Sokaris, there is Death, or the revelations that Death can give. Where Death stalks, light is never far behind.

★

Saqqara was a true city of the dead. To approach it we have to do so via its tutelary deity, Sokaris himself. To a great extent we have no need for any entrance via 'gates' because the Henu Boat itself ensures an entry. The Henu Boat is Sokaris.

When we approach Saqqara using the Nome Standard for Memphis we invariably find ourselves outside the walls of Djoser's pyramid complex, in a strangely modern world of yet more step pyramids and tombs, and vistas of limestone walls, all deeply engraved with those hieroglyphs which guide the dead far more effectively than western script because they reach beyond the brain cells of the merely conscious mind, deep into the psyche itself. If the atmosphere of places can be symbolised by precious metals, then Aunu was polished gold, while Saqqara is old silver. Old silver and the white fire of the moon upon limestone, and numberless pyramids glistening into the night.

The Henu Boat in this instance transforms itself, like a Japanese toy, so that Sokaris stands behind us with Kha'm-uast, for once, absent.

★

Sokaris, who was hailed as 'the great god who came into being in the beginning, he who resteth upon the darkness' can take a variety of forms. He is most usually seen as a man with a falcon head, though this is an altogether more antique creature than the fierce, pitiless bird of Horus. As Lord of the Mysterious Realms, Lord of the Dead and of the Darkness, he is often linked with Set through an arcanum that we will not really understand until we get to Thebes - if then. He is also linked with the Earth-god, Geb, and sometimes even Tem, the Dark Sun. In the earliest of times he was almost exclusive to Memphis, but as that city's power grew so did he. Sometimes he was shown (usually on coffins) as a hawk with the Red Crown of Lower Egypt and plumes upon his head, standing on a low pedestal from the front of which projects a serpent.

Quite often he was so identified with the god Ptah, whom we shall meet very soon, that he became known as Ptah-Sokar; and later still Osiris (Asar) became drawn into his folds to form a Triple God figure known as Ptah-Sokar-Asar. Like the Father, Son and Holy Ghost of the Christians, Ptah-Sokar-Asar was a 'triune god of the resurrection'.

When we envision the latter in his human form he appears in the debatable features of someone who is either quite young, but looks rather old, or else manifests an air of age while looking strikingly young. Lord of the Dead or not, this entity was also associated with virility, energy and fertility, and sometimes even alluded to in crude, ithyphallic dwarf form. In the latter case it is

Figure 10b - The High Priest of Heliopolis >

rather like a modern person conceding that while a certain individual was outwardly a fine, upright citizen, inwardly he was something of a 'dirty old man', or a 'bit of a ram'. This is a case of Egyptians using their arts of statuary and symbolism to express what we would via colloquialisms. Many of the bewildering, multi-faceted aspects of the Egyptian deities can be resolved if looked at in this light.

★

If it is possible (and it is) to turn inward and identify a specific area within the psyche/genes/spirit/subconscious - call it what you will - that contains the essence of all the souls who have helped create us, and raise us, and support us, and who have since passed on (though not necessarily died) then this area of consciousness is Sokaris.

When we feel Sokaris behind us amid the luminous enclosures of Sakkara, we are in the presence of 'the great god who eateth away the soul, who eateth hearts and who feedeth upon offal, the guardian of the darkness' - to quote a desperate petition from Chapter XVII of the *Book of the Dead*. Sokaris can bring terror: the air around us trembles with the slow exercise of his wings; the earth beneath our feet trembles as though a great worm were agitating beneath our feet, and the dead of this world were striving to break upward. He can make us feel like offal ourselves, about to be consumed.

★

There is a technique in magic which can enable us to make use of these feelings and images. It is known as the Assumption of the God-form, and involves the magician visualising himself in the actual shape and posture of the deity whose energies are being utilised. It involves more, however, than merely adopting a stance and projecting a few lines and shapes upon the imagination: like a method actor the magician should also *feel* the qualities of the god or goddess concerned, and *become* the deity in question. In a real sense this is what actually happens when the god 'descends' to do his part.

The best way that we begin with Sokaris is to intone his name, screeching it within our head like a hawk, while visualising ourselves changing into pure hawk shape to soar above a barren landscape, soaring so high that the trees below look no more than loose scrub, trailed with long shadows of the setting sun.

The feel of actually soaring can be enormously effective. This

Figure 11b - The Sem Priest >

hawk-shape is actually the Henu Boat transformed to suit the circumstances. You are within Sokaris. You *are* Sokaris.

At some point you will see what seems to be a small, pink, shrew-like rodent scurrying below, heading to the West. With your phenomenal eyesight you can close in and see it clearly. Naked, desperate, frightened as it is, you can feel no pity when you recognise it as yourself.

Sokaris folds his wings and plummets, screaming down through the atmosphere, down through the levels of consciousness much as the soul once fell past the stars and into matter. Only at the last moment does Sokaris open his wings, extend his claws and snatch up that voiceless and pathetic figure before winging upward again to perch upon the World Tree and consume his prey.

★

It is not an exercise that can be repeated too often. There is a limit to how often a person can or should consume themself, after all. But the important point of the exercise occurs when the Traveller re-emerges from within Sokaris - expanding while Sokaris' phantasm shrinks within him, until the image of the hawk with outstretched wings is left engraven within his heart-centre like some amulet.

The Traveller at this point has balanced his own Death within him. Now he can begin to live with the intensity he should.

★

Many of us have lost our own souls at some time through fear of Death. We have often 'eaten our hearts out' in dread of its coming. The petitioner quoted from the *Book of the Dead* goes on to ask who this dread god is who carries away souls, who eats hearts and feeds upon offal. But we can now snatch the answer from his mouth by taking a single finger, in crude copy of Kha'm-uast's *uas* wand, and point it quite certainly at our own breast bone.

It is only now, tinged by understanding of Sokaris, that we can explore the necropolis in the right manner, while bearing within our hearts the only real message that this ancient god would seek to impose: the most important lesson of death is loving while you are still alive.

★

In effect, Sokaris' kingdom is universal. He is amongst the oldest of gods because Death is amongst the oldest of revelations. Only self-awareness and self-love (Atum) could be said to precede him. Sokaris in the winged form stretches out and curves his plumage around the world to encompass everything, for all things eventually die or decompose in the animal, vegetable and mineral worlds. Each wing - and indeed Sokaris' whole body - is composed of an infinite number of feathers. Each feather on its own is a symbol of Maat, the Cycle of Nature, or the 'World Order', who is also called Truth and Justice. It is therefore true, natural, and part of the ordered basis of life itself that all things are enwrapped at intervals by Sokaris' wings. This is when night comes, and Death appears.

This is when we can find Sokaris striding up and down the vast chain of funerary complexes which stretch for almost fifty kilometres along the West bank of the River Nile, always to the West of the various sites and cities, his early influence taking in the sites of Dahshur, Abu Sir, Abu Ghurab and Giza itself. At some point, however, perhaps wearied by the long march, Sokaris changed into his pure bird form and perched exclusively in that centre which now bears his name if not always his understanding.

The other sites nearby can wait for other Journeys. We all have to visit Saqqara once in our lifetimes.

★

With the power of Sokaris within us, real or imagined (and there is not often a lot of difference in the multi-dimensional realms through which we travel) we can see around the necropolis with that curious kind of night-sight that Death or astral vision can give us: mundane obstacles of landscape are removed: if we cannot gaze upon places by direct line of sight we are still aware of their presence and location. Like a child's painting we can take them all in without perspective, without any narrowing of vision. Unlike Aunu, which we had to study via the fragments of a broken mirror, Saqqara is like a great beetle - a scarab - which is trapped in amber 'forever and forever'.

If we stand at the cross-roads marked in Figure 8, facing West, at a time when the sun has long since settled, we find that Djoser's step pyramid is before us, only the upper layers visible above the high white walls of the surrounding complex; turning on our own 'world-axis' slightly to the left we can see the much smaller but no less influential pyramid of Unas, and sense the tomb of Idut tucked away between that and Djoser's walls. A few degrees more to the left, to the south west of our position, is the unfinished pyramid complex of Sekhemket. Due South are the tombs of Khnum-hotep and Ni-ankh-khnum. Turning all the way around to the north east there is a small pyramid of uncertain provenance, and then the pyramid of Teti with the tombs of Mereruka, Kagemni and Ankh-mahor behind that. Almost due North of us lies the complex of

Userkaf. While to the north-east of us, at an increasing distance, unseen but sensed (much as we can sense the action of our own hearts) is the tomb of Ptah-hotep, beyond which curves the avenue of figures known as the Greek philosophers, while beyond those is the Serapeum, at the north-westerly corner, where the sun was most firmly regarded as having entered the Duat. It is here, in the underground chambers, in another time and dimension, that Kha'm-uast's body will forever lie.

★

In the *ka* posture, in our mind's eye, we can turn and turn, inward and yet more inward, winding in the light. Like the vortex, we draw all things to us. Not yet born as we are, we draw the souls toward us also: Ti, a handsome nobleman of the 5th Dynasty who was Overseer of the Pyramids and Sun Temple, Supervisor of Works, Scribe of the Court, Royal Counsellor and Lord of Secrets, whose wife was the royal princess Neferhotepes; Ptah-hotep, who was Inspector of the Priests of the 5th Dynasty pyramids of Neuserre, Menkauhor and Djedkare; Mereruka, who was a son-in-law of King Teti, from the 6th Dynasty; the high priest and judge Kagemni, and the *ka* priest and physician Ankh-mahor; not to mention the figure of Unas (the last of the 6th Dynasty kings) and the gruff figure of Djoser himself.

In Khem the name of something or someone - the *ren* -   was a means to power in one sense or another, as we shall learn from the priests of Hermopolis. Some of the names have wonderfully evocative sonics with a facility for echoing in our consciousness like the slapping of sandals down a long, temple corridor. Often the very intonation can produce sparks which in themselves can carry the essence of the original consciousness through to us today.

Assuming the form of Sokaris we can summon them up with their actual names as we turn and turn into the space between the worlds. Sometimes they will come - often in the most unexpected ways - sometimes they will not. That is the way of everyday life also. And if not their actual essence at least their echoes or shells, which are formidable enough in themselves and which still have much to teach us. Ti, cultured and urbane, will respond better to women; Kagemni likes those with a very precise, almost niggling cast of mind; Ptah-hotep is often hard to keep away; while Djoser himself counts it no honour to be disturbed.

Sometimes, when the link is made, the Traveller gets odd flashes as to how they view him: *they* see the Traveller from the vantage point of their own time, as old, incredibly old. Often they see him as Sokaris, come to peer at their lives.

And those moments in our own lives, now in the 20th Century, when we are struck by an overwhelming sense of Death's eventual onset, and feel compelled to review our own lives and circumstances, we can imagine that in some world aeons from now a Traveller is also examining us in much the same way as we do here amid the dead of Saqqara.

Time, as all tomb-dwellers know, is a Mobius strip. Time is a rosary through the fingers.

★

The step pyramid of Djoser was, as already mentioned, designed by that extraordinary creature Imhotep, the king's Chancellor, who provided Egyptian architecture with what was essentially a quantum leap toward the stars. He was actually deified, and soon usurped Nefertum's role as a god of creative inspiration. Whoever enters Netjeryket Djoser's pyramid will invariably touch upon the spirit of Imhotep, whose own tomb has not yet been found, and who left his mark upon the present and previous century via the works of Isambard Kingdom Brunel.

The step pyramid was surrounded by a huge wall almost two kilometres long and more than ten metres high. Although there was fourteen great gateways in this wall, all bar one were 'false doors' of the sort that we will come to use ourselves later in the Journey. Inside the complex were replica temples, courts and pavilions, duplicating Djoser's own residence in his lifetime. Stone imitations of open wooden doors were carved where it was possible to enter rooms within; wall panels decorated in blue-glazed tiles which copied the reed mats hung on interior doors, were a common feature; large statues of Djoser in all manner of poses, and domestic treasures of all kinds littered every niche and corner shelf, as they had done in the king's own home. Everything - the workshops, the kitchens, the places of sacrifice and celebration - everything a duplicate in stone or mud-brick or alabaster of that which had once been known to Djoser in his lifetime. Everything built to last for 'millions and millions of years' as the beautiful and often maddening phrase went. And no-one to live there but the ghosts of Djoser and his retinue.

It is rare that Djoser will deign to take the Traveller very far into his complex: it is usually Imhotep who guides the way - Imhotep/Nefertum who is really the spirit of curiosity and the bright idea within us.

Whatever else we might find in that complex, we must first of all find a certain closed room near the north-east corner of the pyramid, behind many closed and jewelled doors, where broods a life-sized statue of the pharaoh himself, with his right arm bent upon his chest, fist clenched, and his left hand flat upon his thigh. His skin is painted gold, his hair is jet black, and his eyes glitter with a fortune in inlaid precious stones. Imagine yourself reaching out and gently touching his lips in a presage of that mysterious Opening of the Mouth ritual that we will learn about in Abydos. Imagine the secrets that this statue could tell if only it could talk. In magical terms such statues were a link between the mortal world and the soul of the deceased, just as the living pharaoh was a link between the mortal world and the gods themselves. Consciousness in flesh or consciousness in stone...the wisdom of the Neters could come through in different ways on different levels in different realms.

We can lose ourselves amid the marvels of Djoser. He knew things about Man and his origins that were only fables by the time of the later pharaohs.

In a sense we have all touched upon the spirit of his pyramid complex during those times when, usually on a high place on a still day, we have looked down upon the world and had the strange sensation that it was all unreal - a painting or an elaborate stage back-drop through which we could crash toward some other reality if only we dared to leap. It is a common enough experience, but exactly the sort that the Traveller will experience when he explores such a place as Djoser's pyramid.

Far more accessible is the strange pyramid of Unis which looks today like no more than a heap of rubble, but which contains those matchless hieroglyphs which became known as the Pyramid Texts. These texts, which were magical directions for the king's progress in the netherworld, became standard features in all later pyramids, built into them like computer programs in the directional systems of modern spacecraft. We enter this one from the North, through an antechamber and past three massive granite slabs, before entering the burial chambers themselves, with their dazzling array of hieroglyphs. The Traveller needs no light here: the symbols burn in his brain, even if he does not consciously understand them.

We can visit the rest of them in much the same way that we visited the Great Pyramid if we so wish: Teti, Pepi I, Mererue and Pepi II; the unfinished complex of Sekhemkhet which hovers even in the astral light like something which is either half-dissolving or half-manifest; Userkaf and Shepseskaf (which is more of a huge mastaba than a pyramid as such); Izezi, Ibi, Merykare and Khendjer; and beyond these the enigmatic but unexceptional pyramid whose owner is still anonymous. Fifteen pyramids and myriad rock-cut tombs and mastabas, taking in all levels of Egyptian society and more of the 'death wisdom' locked away within that comparatively small area than most nations ever accumulate.

The Traveller could go mad in Saqqara if he were not careful. Not because of the ghosts, but because of the frustration. So much to see and learn, with such a short life in which to do it.

We can visit all of the places mentioned and many more which space precludes, but if we are to have any understanding as to *why* there should have been such an overwhelming cult of the dead, we have to follow the long winding causeway which curves to the North and then the north-east, glistening and sometimes seeming to writhe underfoot like the back of a serpent.

We have to visit the Serapeum.

★

In the year 1850 CE, if we are to play the Game of the Neters again, Europe was agog at the prospect of German reunification, and sometimes mightily worried; the Pope had divided England into Roman Catholic dioceses and restored a Catholic hierarchy once more; Foucault's humble little pendulum was clearly demonstrating to some astonished folk the Earth's rotation, while the Earl of Rosse was busy discovering spiral nebulae. In public realms municipal libraries were being established which would bring learning to the common man, while various bright souls from all nations were perfecting the refinement of petrol in a way that would make the internal combustion engine possible and change everything, for all time. Old things were returning, fundamental truths were being discovered, confirmed and disseminated; raw materials were being refined with half an eye upon the stars... In 1850, the 20th Century was being born.

It was in this year that a young Frenchman by the name of Auguste Mariette was sent to Egypt by the Louvre with the specific task of buying Coptic manuscripts from the monasteries. Coptic texts were big news in certain circles in 1850. Possessed by the romance of his mission, however, and taken by the magic of a country that was as yet unspoiled by tourism, he quickly forgot his brief and found himself, within days, at Saqqara. Stretching the rules of the Game of Neters to their fullest then Mariette, whose name might be mistranslated as Smallhusband or even Younghusband, was about to allow a peculiar type of magic to come westward just as the English explorer Francis Younghusband was to prise open and release the Tibetan spirit for the same curious occidentals.

It was here, peeking just above the sand, that he discerned

what seemed to be an avenue of sphinx heads. Remembering Strabo's comments in the 1st Century CE about just such an avenue leading to the fabled temple of Serapis, Mariette wrote: 'At that instant I forgot my mission...I forgot the Patriarch, the convents, the Coptic and Syriac manuscripts and Linant Bey himself...' Pausing only to hire a group of some thirty men, he began the dig at sunrise, 'One of the most beautiful sunrises I had ever seen in Egypt', and didn't slow down until he found the bulls.

And considering the peculiar nature of the energies concerned, it was entirely and unconsciously appropriate that the dig began at sunrise on 1 November, the old pagan festival of Samhain, when the dead were felt to be closer to the world of men than at *any* other time...

★

What Mariette actually found was an underground series of chambers where the sacred bulls of Apis were entombed. These vaults, after the name Serapis, were known as the Serapeum.

Now Serapis was a composite god blending the generative, creative aspects of Ptah and Osiris as they were seen to incarnate in the Apis Bulls, thus forming the Egyptian Asar-Apis, which the Greeks transformed in their usual way as Serapis.

Only certain bulls were chosen for certain periods of time - opinions vary wildly from 14 to 25 years. Each bull had to have certain markings to distinguish its divinity: a white triangle on the brow; the figure of a vulture on the back; a crescent moon on the right flank; the image of a scarab on its tongue; double hairs in its tail.

Each bull was chosen for possessing one or more of these symbols. The search for the new Apis was conducted nationwide. In its lifetime it was worshipped as an incarnation of Ptah himself, and the creative powers of solar fire. In death, like all Egyptian kings, it was assimilated with Osiris and his cyclical, renewing powers.

The rites of the Apis Bulls, like those of the Horned God in Europe, were uninhibited Dionysiac affairs which pounded into orgiastic conclusions under the pale light of the moon, beneath the looming and towering astral form of the Apis Bull himself, presiding over the ceremonies like the great figure of the goat-headed (and very often bull-headed) man who was seen to preside over the witches' dance in Europe. The bull was life in its most rampant and virile, powerful form. Every part of the bull could be used for human benefit: food, medicine clothing...even its shit had wonderful fertilising powers.

During its lifetime the bull was fed in the temple built especially for it at Memphis. When it was turned loose in the courtyard each of its movements could be interpreted as foretelling the future. Not many of the watchers could look the bull in its red and baleful eye. Feeding it was something of a lottery among the younger priests: if it refused to eat, it usually meant bad things for the feeder.

If the bull lived beyond a certain age it was ritually slaughtered. In each case, at death, its body was mummified with as much care and ceremony as that accorded to the king - whose Divine Substitute the bull was. This figure was then placed in a giant sarcophagus made of pink granite, from Aswan, and the cry would go out among the common folk that the Bull was dead - long may he roar.

★

It was the bulls that Mariette was after, but as he cleared away the sand and debris he found empty vault after vault, stretching away down a long corridor, each one looted in previous centuries. It was only when he cleared away a rockfall which had crushed some of the older bull-galleries that he found something else: he found a coffin with a human mummy in it, interred where he had expected a bull to be.

This vault, at least, had not been looted. It had been protected by the earth itself which had smothered the coffin completely, for the earth, surely, knew that Kha'm-uast still had work to do.

Although it was quite badly damaged the mummy still retained its beautiful jewellery. The face was covered with a gold mask. Two gold chains hung around the neck. A golden hawk with outstretched wings lay on the breast, and with it a heart scarab of stone. Lying near the mummy were numerous ushabtis, small figurines which were held to be imbued with protective spirits much like certain bottles were regarded as containing genies. Some of these ushabtis bore the title of Prince Kha'm-uast - who probably needed their assistance less than any other soul upon the planet - but others were for dead Apis, and these would continue to care for and serve the bull in the afterlife as humans had done in this.

★

Compared to the treasures found by other explorers in other tombs, Mariette may have come to feel that his initial excitement was out of all proportion to the actual yield. Some of the finds made their way to the Louvre - the gold mask and some ushabtis, for example;

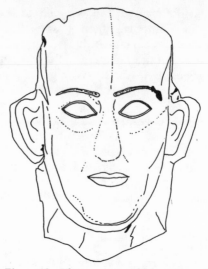

Figure 12 - Kha'm-uast's gold funeral mask

some went to Berlin; and despite a bold piece of misidentification by the Cairo Museum, no-one now knows where Kha'm-uast's mummy ended up - although the likeliest guess is in France.

One important feature of the Serapeum, however, which did manage to survive the centuries of destructive looting, was the 'false door' which is now to be seen in the side chamber of the large crypt, although it had originally sealed off the entrance to the now reconstructed steps which lead to the Small Tombs. Today, the three large fragments, very weathered, are fitted together to make the best of things (in much the same way that we have done in this text), but if we look at them with our inward eye, with our Traveller's eye, this 'false door' can become very real indeed.

These were in fact conventions in all Egyptian tombs from the 2nd Dynasty onwards. Built, some of them, with extraordinary care and attention to detail, they were never meant to open in the earthly sense, and were incapable of being opened except with a large hammer.

Magically, the purpose of these doors was to act rather like the screen of an old television set: if we knew how to work it, if the equipment was still functioning, and if there was appropriate sources of power with proper connections between the two, the *ka* of the departed would come to meet us. To find Kha'm-uast within the Serapeum (or indeed any soul within similar) we have to use this false door within our creative imagination. To those who have been brought up in the television age the time of the 'false door' has

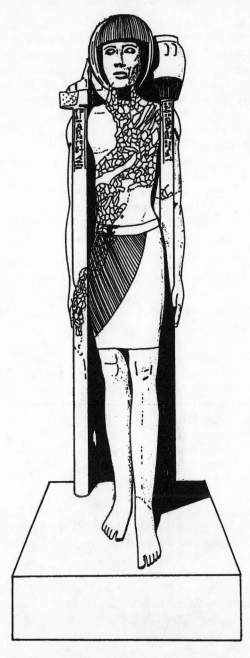

Figure 13 - Kha'm-uast's Monument for Eternity

come round again. The Traveller can use any clear space of wall to create his screen, in lieu of an actual temple. In Kha'm-uast's case the originally blank stone was tuned into his frequency and his alone, by means of hieroglyphic statements. Those Travellers not particular taken with our Guide could do similar by chalking appropriate symbols upon a blackboard which is placed accordingly and used exclusively.

In our case it is not necessary to have an exact understanding of the hieroglyphs shown, but it can help to utter them in translated form while the glyphs themselves sink into our unconscious, apparently forgotten, but all the while channelling inward to make electrical connections between the dream-stuff of the mind and certain brain cells. In fact the fragments are nothing very wondrous, the translation by no means exact, given the extent of weathering on the upper surface, but they read as follows:

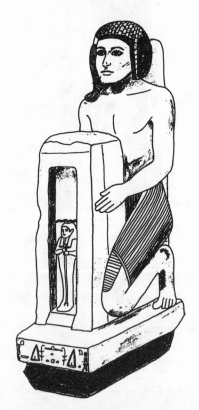

Figure 14 - Broken statue of Kha'm-uast from Memphis

Figure 15 - Kha'm-uast wearing the Sem's wig with the side lock curl

On the right of the outside:

(1)...appearing as Nefertum, the Lotus at the nose of Ra in the eastern horizon; at whose sight the gods renew themselves...for the Sem-Priest and King's Son, Kha'm-uast, in his beauty.

(2)...and all good things which are placed on the altar of Ptah-Sokar, Lord of Saqqara, which is left from the daily offerings to the Chief Artificer, Sem-Priest and King's Son, Kha'm-uast, justified.

On the left of the outside:

(1)...journeying in the morning barque across the heavens, the Sem-Priest and King's Son, Kha'm-uast goes without descending or passing away...

(2)...what heaven gives, the earth brings forth and Nun brings forth from the heights for the Chief Artificer, Sem-Priest and King's Son, Kha'm-uast, justified.

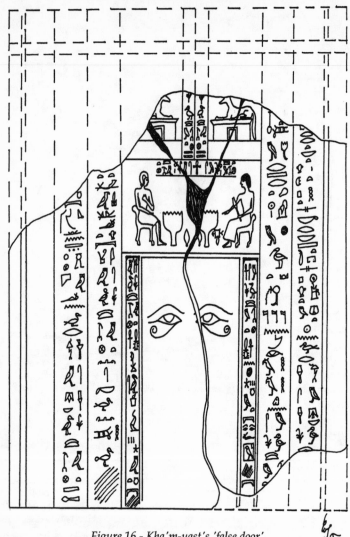

Figure 16 - Kha'm-uast's 'false door'

On the right of the inside:

May the Sem-Priest and King's Son, Kha'm-uast live like the stars live in the sky. May he see Hathor...

On the left of the inside:

May the Sem-Priest and King's Son, Kha'm-uast live like the stars live in the sky.

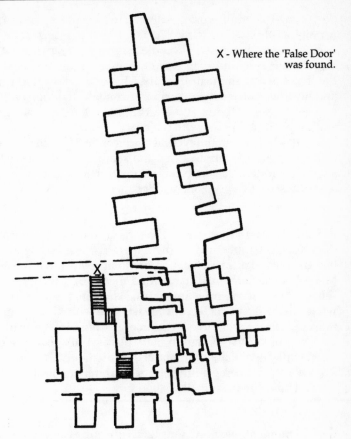

X - Where the 'False Door' was found.

Figure 17 - Map of the Serapeum

After some time exploring Inner Egypt the Traveller does begin to gain some sense as to the message of the hieroglyphs. Not in the manner of picking up clear structures, translations which can be neatly written down, but like those names from our earliest childhood which are not quite remembered, nor yet wholly forgotten: names which stutter on the tips of our tongues and hover maddeningly at the edges of memory, each one attached to floating faces and impulses and chunks of emotional experience which were once the centre of the world, in every person's life before puberty.

Kha'm-uast's false door 'takes' when the eyes become alive. Are they his eyes looking out, or your eyes looking in? It does not really matter. It does not even matter if you simply pretend the experience because that too, like the imitative games of children as they copy the adult world, will enable us one day to grow into certain wisdoms. But if the Traveller is using this door in the magical sense then he will become aware of a steep descent down steps, a left turn and then a right, before he finds himself in the depths of Egypt, in the heart of the Mysteries, alone within a long and northward stretching corridor that stinks of living bulls - that echoes to their pawing and snorting, amid red-purple glowing walls that throb in tune with the heart.

It is here, amid the cyclical spirits of the Horned God, within a corridor full of impulses that the sanitised western world has almost forgotten, that we can meet up with Kha'm-uast again, the Sem-Priest and King's Son, justified...

★

We can dismiss the god-form of Sokaris now, if we have not already done so - preferably by drawing it inwards, and sealing it into the heart centre like a hawk-shaped amulet. Before we can go into Memphis itself we must stand amid these bulls, which are themselves echoes of an earlier animist and shamanic culture, and listen while Kha'm-uast touches our breast bone with his *uas* wand. We must stand for a while and let the energies flow from him to us and back again, in what is the ultimate place of his power. We must listen while he explains more about the rationale of Sakkara, and the Two Ways, and come a little closer to understanding the driving force behind Egypt, and all it stood for.

★

For the moment, we need simply divide our essence into the two aspects of soul and spirit, which we might term the *ka* and *ba* respectively. We will learn a deeper analysis of these when we visit Hermopolis, but for the moment, in these narrow chambers beneath the desert sands, these terms will be quite adequate.

In such crude and hurried terms the *ka* is animated by the *ba*, just as the physical body is animated by the *ka*. It is the Russian Dolls image again.

Upon the death of the physical body the *ka* departs. Consciousness is then contained entirely within the *ka's* structure. After a process of individual revelation based upon a review of all that the individual did or failed to do during his or her lifetime, there then begins a process of 'second death', in which the *ka* degenerates as the body had previously done, and releases the *ba*, which is then absorbed among the neters.

After some time - and time of course is by now completely relative - the *ba* is involved in the process of choosing a new body and manifesting itself in the material world through a new incarnation.

This so far, is fairly standard belief among all those cultures and cults which accept reincarnation as a matter of plain fact.

The Egyptians, however, perceived an alternative. Their seers insisted that as long as the physical body remained, then reincarnation could not take place. The individual would then continue to exist in the Otherworld, the Duat, using the *ka* as his grossest vehicle.

Mummification, therefore, was a means of avoiding the Second Death, as well as demonstrating to those who remained that the true essence of life lies somewhere other than in that dried and empty corpse.

This was not because the mummified entity sought to live on through an eternity of hedonistic delight within the astral plane, but so that it could continue on a higher level as vigorously as it had sought to do on earth.

We are back with Djoser's pyramid again: step by step to the heavens.

And more, because tangible links were still maintained with the souls of the living - via the *ka* statues, the false doors, and trance work of the seers at certain ceremonies, the dead king could still involve himself in the governance of the nation at the level of (literally) spiritual adviser.

The Egyptians, whose psyches still seemed to reverberate with their memories of the Fall, wanted above anything else to maintain their links with *all* the worlds.

There are other parts to the occult constitution of Man as determined by the Egyptians, but they need not concern us yet. It is the Ka, really, which is all important, for the *ka* is in all things, and all things are in the *ka* of Ptah. Whenever we travel in the magical sense, whenever we Journey, it is with the *ka* that we are most profoundly involved.

★

Kha'm-uast, with his *uas* wand on our breast-bone, can teach us many things about our inner nature here amid the bulls, under the earth. He actually uses the wand to push energies and understandings into us, as well as pulling forgotten knowledge out of our own selves. He also knows that if he pushes the wand a *little* further into us, he can touch upon that endocrine gland which is most linked with the heart centre...and that chakra known as the Anahata.

The thymus gland is found in all vertebrate (backboned) animals. In humans it consists of two lobes in the upper chest, behind the breastbone, which in themselves resonate to the two aspects of Sokar and Ptah.

Its role is to do with the body's immunity, stimulating the development of the thymus cells both within itself, and within lymphoid tissue elsewhere in the body. Thymus cells attack foreign substances invading the body, and also control the production of disease-fighting antibodies by other cells of the immune system.

Not surprisingly it was at Memphis that pharaoh kept his standing army in a large garrison just outside the city. Not surprisingly, the tomb and temple decorations were so concerned with using their outer courts and walls to commemorate military victories - particularly Rameses II's triumph at the Battle of Kadesh, which is often detailed *ad nauseum* throughout his monuments.

Just as the thymus gland is responsible for the rejection of transplanted tissues and organs, so was Rameses II famed for driving the foreign invaders off Egyptian soil.

Without the regulating and defensive powers of the thymus (all of which found echoes in the civil, religious, and military structures of Memphis), the growth processes of the thyroid would be negated by disease. Without pharaoh on his throne, at this juncture of the Upper and Lower Kingdoms, then Maat, the Balance of Nature and the Nation, could never hold sway upon the land.

The thymus is actually formed within the human fetus in the first few weeks, developing from two separate segments that join together to create a single organ, as the North and South kingdoms were joined, and pharaohs were always crowned at Memphis. So in a magical sense, if there was illness or despair in Egypt, it was because the pharaoh was not fulfilling his true role.

Like Memphis the thymus is very large in relation to bodily weight in the early years of life, but begins to decline - literally shrink - from puberty onwards. After memphis, Thebes - in the purely historical sense.

Both lobes of the thymus are held together by connective tissue. They are also covered by a dense connective tissue whose branches extend into and separate the lobes into smaller sections known as lobules. Like Egyptian temples and pyramid complexes each lobule consists of an outer zone (cortex) which is divided into an outer cortex and a deep cortex, plus a central inner zone known as the medulla. Inside the medulla are whorls of flattened cells known as Hassall's corpuscles. And it is here, within this biological sanctum, that some cells are destroyed while others are released into the lymph systems to circulate in the body - much as the divine essence of the mummified circulate through the Duat, and thus the consciousness of all Egypt.

The sort of bull-visions that the Traveller might get within the Serapeum are always intensely personal affairs, relating as they do to the individual's sense of power and/or sexuality. Quite often though, visions relating to national or even international concerns may come through but it is never wise to put too much weight on these. Assessing the validity of such things is all part of the Journey, and the Traveller can only do it for himself. Wrestling with bulls, however, in more senses than one, is something that everyone experiences sometime in their lives. In Egypt, many temples carried images which showed the current pharaoh doing just that. If we are to understand this mystic centre more fully, however, we have to enter Memphis itself, either as a direct extension of our visit to Saqqara, leaving the Serapeum at dawn, perhaps, and heading into the rays of the sun to find ourselves before the great gates in the usual fashion; or by riding there on a bull's back; or from our initial launching point within the isle of Khebit while using the symbol of the Nome Standard and the true name of Memphis, which is Men-nefer. All serious Travellers must sort out their own links and connections from any one stage of the Journey to the next.

Men-nefer is a name which derives from the Old Kingdom when Pepi I had his pyramid built at a chosen site in Saqqara. Since he actually had his court within the city this quarter became known as Men-nefer (or nefru)-Mire, which means 'The Beauty of King Mire (Pepi I) Endures'. In time this got shortened to 'Menfe' and applied to the whole city rather than just one portion of it. The Greeks - it was always the Greeks - twisted this into 'Memphis'.

Another of its names was 'Balance of the Two Lands', called thus because Menes, the founder of Dynastic Egypt, situated the city at the traditional borderland between the North and the South, or the Upper and Lower Kingdoms.

It was the original white-washed mud-brick walls of Menes' palace fortress which gave the city its original name - Ineb-Hedj or 'White Walls'. By the time of Kha'm-uast Men-nefer had expanded beyond the original walls to become the foremost city of Egypt, and perhaps the world.

In modern terms the Egyptians of Kha'm-uast's day looked upon Aunu like some kind of Harvard: but Men-nefer was pure Manhattan. It showed in the attitudes too, which we can often pick up when we Journey: the spirit of Aunu was often marked by smugness: that of Men-nefer was big-city arrogance.

At the heart of the sprawl stood the original Ineb-Hedj, the first royal citadel whose white walls had inspired Imhotep to build

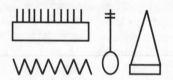

Figure 18 - The symbol for Men-nefer

similar around his tomb masterpiece at Saqqara during the 3rd
Dynasty. However, the city developed to such an extent that quite
apart from the splendid temples and palaces and theological developments that it spawned, it could well have originated the concept
of suburbia also.

The Southern District contained the harbour, Peru-nefer (or
Pernufi), a site of numerous warehouses with ships constantly
coming and going for Men-nefer had international and national
trading links - in which we can glimpse the circulatory action of the
thymus. The immensely crowded foreign quarter here, especially
during the New Kingdom and Late Period, was home to Phoenicians,
Greeks, Jews, Persians, Hittites, Carians, and Syrians, among others. Each ethnic group had its own separate quarter, and also
temples and shrines to their native deities, among which was Baal
and Astarte. Such a rich mixture of nationalities was reflected in
songs and poetry which mention Men-nefer's international inhabitants.

The Southern District was also the site of Pharaoh's large
standing army which fulfilled the protective/aggressive aspects of
this the thymus centre of Khem. While it was here, also, that the
industrial areas were located - shops, factories, warehouses plus
homes for what we would now call the 'blue-collar' workers. It was
here too that Hathor, whom we shall meet later, was most passion-
ately worshipped.

To the North and the East of the city was the business and
administration area, suitably known as 'The City', which also
boasted a smart residential quarter of fine houses and well-tended
gardens for its inhabitants. Just to the West of the City was the
District of Pharaoh where the royal residences stood, a great ram-
bling palace like some old and elegant hotel, where visiting royalty
were wont to stay. This palace was sometimes called 'the Domain
of Akheperkare'. In addition to all this both Seti I and Rameses II
kept their own harems within the city, as well as their own royal
residences.

The area that Kha'm-uast spent most of his time was in the
District of Ptah, which contained the massive Temple. The latter

had simple enough origins, but was expanded over the centuries until it required its own district to contain all its properties and priests. Rameses II, carrying on with this tradition, had a grand new Jubilee Hall built for himself on the Temple's West side. Here, amid towering columns behind a pylon gateway and its monumental statues, the Heb-Sed Festival was carried out, often with Kha'm-uast as his father's proxy, ratifying the king's fitness to rule, bringing order and peace within the spirit of the land throughout each of the Nomes.

The Temple of Ptah was important to the kings of Egypt because it was here that they came for the coronation ceremonies. This tradition reflects the fact that the first king of a united Egypt, Menes, had himself crowned with the Double Crowns at Men-nefer. Even in later centuries, when the 'thymus' role of Men-nefer began to decline after Egypt's historical puberty was reached and Thebes began to dominate, even conquering foreign kings came to Men-nefer for their crowning ceremonies, the most famous example of this being Alexander the Great who, in 332 BCE, after defeating the Persians, rode triumphantly into Egypt and headed straight to Men-nefer to be crowned king of the Upper and Lower Kingdoms, in the Temple of Ptah. Like transplanted tissues, the foreigners knew that once they had the thymus behind them, they stood a chance.

★

Almost nothing remains of Men-nefer today. Once, Rameses II had a great jewel-studded gate built onto the Temple of Ptah, of which he said in a surviving inscription: 'Its doors are like the horizon of heaven'. Once, he had a special shrine to Ptah built, to which his son Kha'm-uast erected two giant statues of his father at the entrance of the temple's southern gate. Now, in the little modern village of Mit Rahina it is only these latter which have survived, and the once-fabled door no more than a potential within our spirit which only Ptah himself can unlock.

★

The priests of Ptah in Men-nefer were servants of their god in a way that is often not easy to comprehend today. The difference lay in the perceptions which the ancient priests possessed then which only a few modern souls can match. These perceptions were part and parcel of their service. The details of how the Egyptian priesthood was organised, the entrance requirements, their obligations and restrictions placed upon them, the different ranks and their overall duties is beyond our scope at present. For now we can, in our imagination, assume the *ka* posture face to face with Kha'm-uast, palms and brows lightly touching, and learn a little more about his own role as Sem.

★

Kha'm-uast had to begin his life in the priesthood of Men-nefer at the bottom rank and work his way up just like anyone else - Crown Prince or not, and despite the fact that the senior priests recognised him as a rare soul of exceeding wisdom.

He started his work in the Temple of Ptah as a we'eb (or wab, uab), the title for 'pure one', the lowest order of priests. This was not really purity in the moral sense, but as a clean sheet, a blank slate. As we'eb he had to sweep the corridors, feed the temple's animals and clean up after the bulls, taking that natural fertiliser to gardens or the pharmacies; he had to be on call to assist any priest of a higher rank; he had to attend all ceremonies, and give what simple ministrations to the populace that his lower rank obliged.

When he first entered the temple the High Priest of Ptah was named Huy, a stocky and genial sort who nevertheless had a disconcerting sense of humour as far as the we'ebs were concerned. It was Huy who presided over the burial of the first Apis Bull in Year 16 of Rameses II's reign. It was Huy whom Kha'm-uast most remembered and most modelled himself after, even when he was succeeded by Pahemneter and Didia, both of whom respected Kha'm-uast (they had to) but neither of whom had quite as much affection for the prodigy as old Huy.

When Kha'm-uast assumed manhood and the full status of Initiate, he resurrected the peculiar title of Sem, to indicate his particular priestly function. It was a title that was archaic even then, as we have already noted, and although it would be nice to speculate on the word *sem* being an ultimate linguistic root of the word 'shaman', the word most likely to sum up the ring which sem had in the ears of Kha'm-uast's predecessors in the temple is that of 'wizard', from the root meaning 'wise'. The term wizard to the 20th Century ear is one of those archaisms which has taken its place within the literary genre of mythological fantasy, but has never really been used by serious modern magicians. While many of these are almost queuing up to describe themselves as 'shamanic', their systems by and large preclude this art in its truest sense. Really they are wizards: they are *Sems*.

In temple and tomb reliefs the Sem priest is usually shown wearing his leopard skin stole around his shoulders and draped over his vestments; this skin was worn by other priests as well but it had a particular association with the Sem, because of the leopard's affinity with the Land of the Dead, in Egyptian tradition. The wearing of this animal's skin allowed the Sem power to deal with the souls of the dead. He wore it at Saqqara all the time.

The other distinctive feature of the Sem priest was the side-lock, or plait, which again had archaic origins. It is thought that in the earliest periods the Sem had been one of the titles and duties of the ruler's eldest son and heir. Such Sem princes were 'helpers', i.e. representatives or mediators of and for their fathers, these duties preparing the prince for his role as king. By Dynastic times, when royal princes were installed in the priesthood, the title gradually shifted onto non-royal priests until it became more a sacerdotal title and duty than that of a princely responsibility.

The Sem was the chief officiant in the 'Opening of the Mouth' ceremony, an enormously long and complex rite in which links were established (or renewed) with the soul of the departed king by means of what we now call a mediumistic trance, but backed up by an elaborate ceremonial which ensured that this was performed not just for the personal benefit of the surviving relatives, but for the guidance and furtherance of the Egyptian psyche as a whole. 'The Opening of the Mouth' ceremony, like those foliate heads often seen on English church carvings, ensured that from the 'mouth' or communicative powers of the dead pharaoh, life and fertility and growth could still spring forth.

★

We can enter the Temple of Ptah by the southern gate between the massive statues of Rameses II, Kha'm-uast leading the way through vast and jewel-studded doors which were pulled open by eager we'ebs; and as each door opens the sound of the singing beyond surges louder, as men and women in white robes and neat lines, each one scrubbed and purified, perfectly rehearsed, sing a great song like the ocean, increasing as a series of the double doors are opened before your path, so that the noon light from behind surges in almost as though you and Kha'm-uast have carried it on a platter. It is a song of the elements and their origins that is so familiar, so old, that you feel like a foetus in the womb, hearing the heart beat and the blood surge around you knowing that soon, soon, you will enter into a still brighter light and look with unfocussed eyes upon your parents' faces.

You only pause at the final door, sealed with Ptah's name, which stretches from the black and white tiles of the floor to the high ceiling where stars can be seen, painted silver upon blue, and the long melting lines of ancient sky-goddesses who beckon you to join them - women without names, long-forgotten but all-forgiving despite that.

Pause at the final double doors. Smell the incense, the distant waft of cooked meat from the sacrificial offerings made earlier, brought in on the rhythmic breezes created by the great semi-circular fans wielded in strict sequence by the we'ebs. Note the strange, clear smell of many people who have washed so often and so thoroughly with pure water that they actually reek of it. Then look at that seal again. Only Kha'm-uast as High Priest can break that seal, although you are allowed to finger the wax, and the images for Ptah. The moment he does so, using the head of his *uas* wand as a lever, the singing stops, the doors swing noiselessly open.

And here, before a statue of Ptah which is suffused with that god's essence, you can sit and listen to those tales which have become known as the Memphite Theology...

★

The main features of the Memphite Theology were preserved by being carved upon a block of basalt now known as the Shabaka Stone, by a king from the 25th Dynasty. According to this, the god Ptah existed before everything else, and had his being in Nun, the primeval ocean which features in most Egyptian cosmogonies. Ptah manifested his creative activities through the intermediary of eight forms 'which existed in him'. This is not so far removed from that god of the Old Testament who created the world in seven stages known as days. Most of these forms have now been forgotten; some of them are being filled in by speculations concerning Man's extra-terrestrial origins.

Ptah is normally represented by a mummified figure, raised on a pedestal, his skull enclosed in a tight head-band and his body swathed in mummy wrappings. Only his hands are free, and these hold a sceptre which unites the emblems of life, stability, and power.

Ptah was the patron of artisans and artists, the inventor of the arts: creative impulses achieving physical expression. He was hailed as, 'the very great god who came into being in the earliest time, father of fathers, Power of powers, father of beginnings and creator of the eggs of the Sun and Moon, lord of Maat, king of the Two Lands...'

Men-nefer, being the link between the Upper and the Lower, was a natural place to find Ptah, known also as the Opener. It is his role to open the doors of perception between that which we know, and that which we don't know. We can invoke his presence every time we open a door and step into a strange room. Although his name has sometimes been translated to mean 'door', he is not the door as such, but *the space between* - whether this is between rooms, levels of consciousness, or modes of being.

Ptah was also, on another level, responsible for fashioning the *ka* of each individual.

★

The difficulty of studying Egyptian religion is that most try to do so all at once, making cross-references and drawing parallels, always seeking to discern the single truth from which all the other cosmogonies sprang. It is actually possible for any Traveller to achieve his own revelation in this respect, but it is never easy and rarely wise to try. Egyptian religion covered thousands and thousands of years, each god and goddess assuming many forms under the influence of many religious movements and/or foreign invasions, and each form developing many positive and negative aspects which responded in differing ways to different people.

It is impossible to be dogmatic about how the gods of different theologies relate and blend. All we can really do when we enter each centre is return our minds to nothingness, to Nun, and start each visit with the open mind of an innocent visitor. We must, in short, become like the we'eb.

★

Ptah, then, was the creator god. He functioned on all levels of the creative act. High Priests at Memphis, in this respect, bore a title which was analogous to 'Master Builder', which hints at Kha'm-uast's involvement in certain occult freemasonic circles this century. Thus when Kha'm-uast did any purely *practical* work - building, carving, painting - he would, at the completion of anything particularly skilled and pleasing, offer the achievement to Ptah. In time, the skills and perceptions which enabled him to achieve this level of work, would begin to link with this particular sonic. On future occasions Kha'm-uast (or anyone) could actually summon up these quality responses before the work began, or in times of practical difficulty. Brain cells would be stimulated; the spirit of Ptah summoned; energies would be exchanged between one plane and another.

Working with Ptah, we can all become 'Master Builders' in whatever field we choose. And whatever we happen to create will be imbued with 'soul' - with *ba*.

★

The theology of Men-nefer was an extraordinary achievement. It acknowledged the deities of Heliopolis and Hermopolis, surely, but with the arrogance of Memphites secure in their ascendancy, they made these distinctly subordinate.

Ptah, they insisted, underlay all things. Ptah was a spirit which was everywhere, and manifested itself through the *ka*, which all things contained. Ptah was the 'Hidden One, whose eternal form is unknown, Lord of the Years, giver of life at will', according to a later text.

Nothing like the Ptah-concept existed in the world until New Testament times.

From Ptah (which can often be effectively uttered as a spitting sound), came Intelligence and Command, sometimes called Heart and Will. The two are complementary: intelligence without application is pointless: applying effort or giving 'commands' is useless without intelligence. Intelligence stemmed from the heart, Command from the tongue. They were linked with Horus the Sun God and Thoth the Moon God, respectively.

It was Ptah-hotep, whose tomb lies in Saqqara, who wrote:

'The seeing of the eyes and the breathing of the nose bring messages to the heart. The seeing of the eyes, the hearing of the ears, and the breathing of the nose bring messages to the heart. It is the latter which causes all decisions to be made, but it is the tongue which reports what the heart has thought out. Thus is all action...carried out - the manipulation of the hands, the movement of the legs and the functioning of the limbs. All is in accord with the commands which the heart has devised and which has appeared on the tongue. Thus is determined the peculiar nature of everything.'

Women, in particular, who have lost their heart to the idea of Kha'm-uast, and thus Ptah, can invoke them both in the plaiting of hair - either literally or in the imagination. Either to their lovers, to themselves, or (assuming the role of Sekhmet here) to their children. The symbol 𓏙 is not only the letter 𓋲 from Ptah, but also Kha'm-uast's side-lock, the feature of the Sem.

Ptah is the spirit which underlies all life, which creates life. Sekhmet, however, is that which protects these creations at all cost. Like one of the functions of the thymus, she will reject and/or destroy anything which might threaten her domain.

The death or Sokar-experience may well have much to teach everyone, but there is a limit even to that kind of revelation. While the Sekhmet *spirit* arose after Ptah, it was clearly the women of Mennefer who created her form. Living as they did alongside the vast line of necropolises, trying to raise their babies in a world that was harsh enough as it was without having the great shadow of the bird-headed man (Sokar) flapping near them, they created the perfect champion: they created Sekhmet, a cat-headed woman. Bird vs. Cat, Hawk vs. Lion, Male vs. Female - a curious balance was imposed upon the world, and a curious kind of magic created for those who understand that sort of thing.

Sekhmet has two aspects, both of them solar: like her consort she is linked with great practical skills, but particularly in the handling of disease. Her skills, however, were more related to the methods of surgery than those which involve tender loving care. In her other aspect (not so far removed) she was quite happy to kill in order to protect, and would do so without any long, agonies of conscience. This, of course, is the spirit of the great cats.

Clearly, like any Egyptian deity, the matter of gender is ultimately symbolic, because her spirit can be invoked (and often was) by any father going to war in order to protect his family. Indeed, some of Sekhmet's statues actually show 'her' with an ithyphallic male body.

She is, then, life in its proudest, fieriest and often most aggressive aspect. When a person can stand upon a high place under a bright sun and exalt at being alive, and in the flesh, and almost drunk with it all, clenching his fists toward the heavens in unconscious use of the *ka* posture, then it is Sekhmet who roars within.

But, however you approach her, whenever, first make sure that Sokar is made very tiny indeed, and well-locked away from her peculiarly teasing, and sometimes tearing energies.

★

Nefertum is born each morning from the lotus, within which the sun took refuge each night. Or in other words consciousness retreats at intervals into that strange dream-world of sleep, from which we can all emerge with unusual experience, and insights. Nefertum is seen whenever an artist or scientist actually wakes from sleep with a new vision or a problem clarified. He is often portrayed in human form holding that curved sword known as the *khepesh*, which indicates that power of unconscious mentation which can cut right through the obstacles and get to the heart of the matter with a single thrust. He is also shown with the lotus sceptre, or else actually emerging from the lotus blossom, and in this respect he is regarded as the patron of perfumes and aromatics. This is not because of any cosmetic, romantic associations, but because the power of smell (almost atrophied today) can link us with the certain areas of the mid-brain and the memory cells more effectively than anything. Smells can evoke hitherto forgotten memories and emotions with great and unexpected suddenness. That, again, is Nefertum emerging from the lotus. The Egyptians understood aromas and their effect upon consciousness to a degree that is almost lost to us today. They lived with Nefertum daily, in more than one sense. We can invoke him every time we sniff.

Ptah, Sekhmet and Nefertum are all that remain of the Memphite ennead, but they are no less potent for all that. As long as Ptah is acknowledged (who provides the *ka* in all things), then all things can be recovered - one way or another.

In a sense there are six Memphite deities out there beyond space and the modern consciousness which are still waiting to be remembered, still waiting for certain doors to be opened so that they can re-enter our world and exert their full influence once more. At another level these are the nodes of consciousness which will help us cope with the devastations caused by certain attitudes, diseases, physical, mental, ecological and spiritual imbalances that are peculiar to the present day.

Now, on the edge of the 21st Century, Saqqara is still in a surprisingly good state of preservation, although its tutelary deity (and thus our personal revelation) of Sokar is scarcely known and least understood in the modern Western world. At Men-nefer in the present village of Mit Rahina, very little remains of the actual buildings, the once-splendid temples and courts, but Sekhmet in her most fierce and war-like role is often rampant throughout the world, particularly in the lion's native home of Africa.

The key to it all is in Ptah. The more we can 'remember' him and touch upon his *ka*. (and thus the *ka* which underlies everything) the more that this particular Centre will restructure itself, and Maat come through to Aeon once more.

That is the point of Ptah.

That is the point of our Journey.

6

HERMOPOLIS

In the whole of Egypt, no centre was more bewildering than Hermopolis. On magical levels, no place harder to get to. Its modern name is El-Ashmunein, but in the ancient world it bore the name - curious even to Egyptian ears - of Khemnu, meaning the City of Eight.

The actual site of Khemnu, today, contains less in the way of remains than almost any other centre in Egypt, excepting the solitary column at Heliopolis. Although it stands in a broad and fertile area of the River Nile's valley, only the merest fragments of temples survive above the general rubble.

Up until 1820 there were still two rows of columns from the hypostyle hall of Thoth's temple, although these dated back only as far as Alexander. To the South of these was found an earlier pylon of Rameses II, in the foundations of which were hundreds of blocks from the dismantled temples of that dismal entity Akhenaten; while elsewhere there is the entrance to a temple of Amenemhet II, and a fragment from a temple of Amun dating back to the 19th Dynasty and Seti II...but not much more.

Rubble and mud is the basis of Khemnu today.

A few miles to the West, near Tuna el-Gebel, is the site of Khemnu's necropolis, and also the catacombs dating back to the Persian king Darius I, which were actually devoted to burials of the sacred ibis and baboon...but little more than that.

On any level you approach it, the spirit of Khemnu is very hard to find.

★

We can enter Khemnu with the hare, which is the  on the standard of this the 15th Nome of what is now Upper Egypt, or the South, that area itself coming under the aegis of the Vulture as opposed to the Serpent.

It is with the hare itself that we can actually gain a clue: that strange creature of madness and leaping and great procreative powers and - as far western folklore goes - of witches and spells and tides of luck, and dances beneath the moon.

We can actually ride into Khemnu on the hare's back if we want, though if we are to see any more than shadows then we have to adopt something of the hare's vision and look at the place with eyes that are more animal than human.

★

Eight deities were worshipped in Khemnu and we have their names at least: Nu and Nunet, Amun and Amunet, Heh and Hehut, Ke and Kekut. Four pairings of male and female.

That at least is a start. Once a Traveller has access to a name, a *ren*, then he can begin to look for introductions.

According to the devotees of the Hermopolitan Recension, these were possibly the oldest gods and goddesses in Egypt, although by now we will have heard that refrain in almost every place visited. Yet in the case of Khemnu there may be some justification in this claim. All of the main centres can feel old, but none of them quite match the overwhelming sense of antiquity projected by this shadowy City of Eight, as the name translates. According to some, the original mound from which Egypt sprung was supposed to have appeared here. Sometimes, when you stand amid the phantoms and hear the wild cries of the sacred birds and beasts, and feel the hair rising on the back of your neck as a direct response to the surge of adrenaline, it is possible to believe it without question.

The deities were grouped into four pairs which carried the titles Night, Obscurity, Secret and Eternity, and bore the heads of frogs and serpents, although cats sometimes appeared also. The goddess Nunet, for example, was sometimes shown with the head of a cobra surmounted by a disk, and sometimes with the head of a cat. Sometimes Heh is serpent-headed, other times he is pure frog. Looking into the hierarchies of Khemnu is like staring too intensely into the darkness outside our homes: eye muscles weaken; fixed objects seem to shift; the familiar and expected can transform themselves into anything.

We can give a notional and debatable tabulation as follows, bearing in mind that in truth the deities of Khemnu writhe together like vipers mating in a nest, and it is always difficult to see where one ends and another begins:

Nu/Nunet	*Amun/Amunet*	*Heh/Hehet*	*Ke/Keket*
Abyss	Hidden Ones	Obscurity	Darkness
Eternity	Secret	Inertness	Nothing
Infinity	Invisibility	Mist	Night
Matter	Energy	Time	Space

The list can be endless, but it cries out for at least one interpretation: Out of the Abyss, in the Mists of Night, the Hidden Ones emerged.

While on another level far down the scale of manifestation, on animal levels of symbology, we could say that from their hollows in the mists of night, the hares emerge...

Khemnu is an atmosphere rather than a doctrine. A place where wisdom is attained through inversions, much as Alice found when she stepped through the looking glass. Other recensions emphasised an androgyne deity emerging with a cosmic burst of light and consciousness to take his place upon the land, but Khemnu emphasised the opposite of these qualities. In the crude sense, the priests of Khemnu knew that without darkness we could not appreciate light; without nothingness we could never have somethingness; without not-knowing we could never have true gnosis.

The Shu Texts of the First Intermediate Period (which were known to be heavily influenced by Khemnu) preserved the phrases: 'in the infinity, the nothingness, the nowhere and the dark', and also, 'where the Universal Lord dwelt when he was in the infinity, the nothingness and the listlessness', and again: 'when the Waters spoke to Infinity, Nothingness, Nowhere and Darkness'.

All of which once more allude to the concept of Nun, or Absolute Nothingness, developing a 'centre' from which manifestation proceeded.

It was from the writhing, cosmic mating dance of the Ogdoad that a primeval egg was formed from which a bird of light burst forth saying: 'I am the Soul, the creation of the Primeval Waters...my nest was unseen, my egg unbroken.' This was the Great Cackler - perhaps the origin of the esoteric notion that the Universe began with a raucous shout of laughter.

There are strong elements of Khemnu in that concept which holds that man has no soul (in the modern sense of the word), only a potential. This potential is comprised of dark and primitive aspects. Only by working on these can a true spark be developed. Only through inner work and suffering, and the confrontation with the darkness, can we begin to shine.

★

Even that is not *exactly* right. But amid the shadow-temples of Khemnu it is as near as the Eight will allow for the moment.

★

After the hare it is the ibis which can take us a little further into the city.

To the Egyptians, the ibis was a perfect symbol for their nation because its white plumage showed the sun, its black neck the shadow of the moon, its body a heart, its legs a triangle, and it always appeared at the rising of the Nile. The ibis relates to Thoth in the same way that the falcon relates to Merlin.

The name Thoth is a corruption of Djehuti, or Tahuti, whom the Greeks identified with Hermes - hence Hermopolis. In this area of Egypt he was seen as a Moon God, intimately connected with tides, and madness and matings, and wisdom of a reflective sort, whose sacred animals were the ibis itself, of course, and also the baboon, which in some households was kept as a pet, trained to pick fruit and even help with simple domestic chores. As one who rescued the Eye of Horus after it was stolen by Set, Thoth is in Khemnu to ensure that the shadow-aspects of this centre do not lose touch with the light entirely.

Thoth appears in many guises throughout the vast array of Egyptian mythology, and although he was respected and admired he never quite attained the public appeal of the likes of, say, Sekhmet and Hathor. Many of the gods began their theological careers as philosophical concepts which, sometimes, attached themselves to human figures from myth or history. Christ was seen in Jesus, Geb in Osiris, but this process never developed with Thoth. He was always the Teacher, Assessor, Communicator, Interpreter, Balancer and Reflector of (Moon) Wisdom.

In any case Egyptian symbology appealed to the masses through the ages in differing ways at differing times. We can best understand this in the modern microcosm of the cinema and the concept of Hero. At its simplest, Hero was enormously handsome, wore a white hat and lived by black and white rules. As the decades (and perhaps the decadence) progressed, Hero became more complex, and sometimes even ugly. He became Anti-Hero or Reluctant Hero, and functioned in a variety of realms beyond that of mere adventure: sexual, intellectual, political, romantic or moral...each role backed up by the appropriate visual and musical symbolism.

The Ancient Egyptian would have understood Hollywood only too well. The Ancient Egyptians actually invented the dream factories.

And so the role of Thoth in Khemnu, surrounded by these strange deities from the primordial mud and slime, is not quite the same as the Thoth from other centres. This one is more concerned with that basic law of Nature which states: Learn - and learn fast. He is concerned with man rising from the animal and herd-responses without in any way rejecting or scorning the potency of these. Thoth knows how we are put together; who better than him to teach us about the *ka*, the *ba*, and the *khaibit*. It is the latter, indeed, which is his own special concern in Khemnu. It is the latter which we can adequately translate as - the Shadow.

★

Although Kha'm-uast would have identified eight aspects to the occult constitution of each individual, in the strange world of Khemnu we need only concentrate upon three:

The *ka* was the basis of everything. It was linked with what we would now term the personality, but it involved more than that. Like the personality, which seems to be given to us at birth like a rolled-up scroll containing our possibilities, the *ka* has determining factors built into it. Like the muscles of the arm, the *ka* ⊔ (and the personality) can be developed. Just as the arms are the means by which we control and manipulate the material world, and the personality the way that we relate to society, so is the *ka* the means by which we can progress.

Placed vertically, the arms of the *ka* reach toward something beyond the mundane world, toward the gods themselves. Placed horizontally, as the breast-muscle structure in the glyph indicates, the *ka* is the means by which we embrace and relate to other living beings - human or animal.

In many cruder texts the *ka* is linked with male generative power and (indirectly) with epithets such as the 'Bull of Truth', and 'Victorious Bull'. Today we might echo this when we ask someone if they have the balls to do something particularly risky; in Khem, they ask the same person if they have a strong *ka*.

Of course not everyone *has* much in the way of a personality, or *ka*. In these cases they often compensate by filling the void with the fundamentalist aspects of religion instead, or submerge themselves within herd or mob mentalities. Not much in the way of balls among this lot. Not much in the way of *ka*. But it is the way that we can all go with a weak *ka* and a strong *khaibit*.

The *ka* itself is dependent upon the Heart and the Name. The symbol of the Heart is  which is another glyph of dual associations. First, it is an obvious pitcher which can respond to the usual imagery such as 'my heart is filled with...'; and second it can be seen as a simple representation of the actual organ, with the apparent handles being truncated valves and arteries.

The *ab* was regarded as the centre of Intelligence. The *ab* sent impulses throughout the body via the blood. The intelligence concerned is that particular spark which enables us to survive in this world by sheer awareness.

The symbol of the *ren*, or Name, is a mouth above water, recalling those obscure kabbalistic traditions in which initiates would only utter the Divine Name with their lips only just above actual water, in an echo of God speaking upon the Face of the Waters. The *ren* is our ability to define the world, to bring into focus those perceptions discerned by the *ab*. In the most banal sense, we can catch a glimpse of the *ren's* power when we find ourselves struggling to find a piece of equipment in a hardware store, and only able to describe it to the proprietor in the most general terms. If we knew its name, its *ren*, we could deal with the situation in a portion of the time.

★

The *ka*, which functions via the *ab* and *ren*, then, also has the *khaibit*, which is known as the Shadow and portrayed quite simply as that.

The *khaibit* is that complex of quirks, cruelties, weaknesses and miserable human failings that we all come into this world with, just as surely as we bring the *ka*. Like the *ka*, the *khaibit* can be developed. Often this does nothing more than bring ill to the others for the temporary benefit of the self. But the *khaibit* can also, like Set, teach us where the sun is.

It is in Khemnu, the shadow-place upon the inner planes, where we can learn about the primitive aspects within us. It is through these aspects that we can often touch the greatest sources of personal drive and magical effectiveness. All those 'Cults of the Shadow', those small and secret and (often) sexually-oriented groups and movements which seek to achieve enlightenment and a queer kind of purity by exploring the dark places of the psyche -

all these are touching upon the Lovecraftian, subterranean aspects of Khemnu. It is here that we often meet the Dweller on the Threshold, that entity of bestial terror on the inner planes that we all have to confront, and ultimately master, only to find that we have been battling a complex comprised of our own atavistic qualities.

How to deal with the Dweller, or the *khaibit*, has always been a major concern of all those who seek the light.

★

The symbol of the *ba* is:

A man-headed bird which inverses the usual symbolism. The *ba* is perhaps more closely related to the ideal of the 'Higher Self' which is part of each individual and yet removed from the world. Crudely speaking, the *ba* inhabits the *ka*, as the *ka* inhabits the *khat*, or physical body. Yet, like the Higher Self, the *ba* is held to belong more truly among the neters.

The *ka* incarnates; it rarely reincarnates. Reincarnation in the popular sense, in which Miss V. dies and then is reborn again with all of Miss V.'s *ka*, *ba* and *khaibit* occurs less often than imagined. Reincarnation in that sense is not universal. Some *kas* never do anything more than decompose - often within the lifetime of a person who has completely failed to develop any kind of spark.

It is the *ba*, or a portion of it, which is involved in the reincarnation process, learning about the material world by incarnating itself a little bit at a time. Thus several individuals, spread across the world and throughout history, can be linked by the same *ba*, joined to it like puppets on a string. When we fly up to the levels of our own *ba*, we can often glimpse these other aspects, and imagine them to be ourselves in former lives.

In rare cases, amongst what the Tibetans would call the 'twice-born', this may very well be true. But by and large it is not so much that we have former lives, as *other* lives.

After death the whole complex of consciousness finds itself loose within the 'double', the *ka*. In due course the 'Second Death' occurs in which the essence of consciousness, the *ba*, withdraws and enters the clear white light of beyond, leaving the *ka* and the *khaibit* to degenerate in the proper way. However, intense emotions at the point of death can often hold the latter two together, and it is as though the *khaibit* forms a hard carapace which prevents the *ba* from making its departure or its own essence felt. This is what occultists term an 'earth-bound spirit' whose impulses are based upon fear, ignorance, or even lust for power.

In almost all ancient cultures there was the stipulation that young people on the edge of puberty (or the Thebes influences in our present scheme) should enter adulthood by means of initiation.

The true essence of initiation, however, is not to be found in any occult ceremonial (no matter how awesome this might be) but in the achievement of some difficult but not impossible task, thus exercising the Heart and Will in the truest and fullest of ways.

Certain young we'ebs from Memphis would be sent to Khemnu (often to work on the phobic aspects of their personalities), so that they would also learn to come from 'nothing and nowhere', and take back a spark of a very special kind. The fact that so many of the sacred places in Khemnu were subterranean should give some clues to this. While today we can - *just* - catch a very distant echo of Khemnu's spirit in the proliferation of all those cults of an animist nature, including those ostensibly bizarre sects which focus upon the control of deadly snakes through means of a purified soul.

This is not a path that everyone can follow. But then Khemnu was not a place that everyone wanted to visit.

The actual priests of Khemnu, like the baboons they tended, were often seen as great tricksters. Some of them of course were just crass, and little more than that, but at best the crude and childish and often elaborate jokes played upon the neophytes were intended to invert the normal senses so that they never knew what to expect, and had to start activating those 'learn-and-learn-fast' survival responses within them just to get through the day.

In Khemnu, the *khaibit* was most intensely alive. All the darkness within an individual was brought to the surface and examined in Khemnu.

★

It is at the inner levels of Khemnu that we touch upon the adrenal glands, situated at the upper pole of each kidney. We can actually imagine Kha'm-uast using the Set-head of his *uas* wand to gouge a channel down through our *ka*, so that the pituitary, pineal, thyroid, thymus and adrenal glands are actually linked, like seeds within a ploughed furrow, awaiting the waters. Yellowish in colour, the right adrenal gland is triangular, and the left crescent-shaped. Each consists of an outer part (cortex) and an inner part (medulla) . They regulate the salt and water metabolism and the neuromuscular function.

This is the gland which is actually responsible for the secretion of epinephrine (also called adrenaline) and norepinephrine, at the behest of the pituitary. Among other things they effect heart rate, blood pressure, and respiration - Heart and Will on another level. They are also responsible for that phenomenon which - literally - causes the hair to stand on end, invariably when the individual feels themself to be in the presence of something unknown and unnameable from dread supernatural realms. In more hirsute epochs, the whole of our body fur would have stood on end.

Just as Khemnu (and Thoth in his role as Initiator) are responsible for helping man to 'wake from sleep' by questioning and overturning his perceptions of reality and the norm, so do these hormones help us awake every morning from a night of unconsciousness. Khemnu was responsible for the Nile's magical current flowing through the Egyptian psyche with appropriate pressure. Whatever 'impurities' were developed during the ostensibly dark practices were filtered clean by those Thoth-developed agencies which paralleled the function of the kidneys.

Just as the occasionally bizarre spirit of Khemnu eventually transferred itself to Alexandria, so today are misfunctions of the adrenal glands dealt with by (among other options) the irradiation, or the complete removal, of the pituitary itself.

★

It is through adrenaline, of course, that we discover those unconscious responses known as 'fight or flight', which is an adequate description of man's choices when reduced to this most primitive level. Tied in with the corollary of 'Learn - and learn fast', it is all a question of whether we survive or whether we die. These are the most basic responses needed to cope with and eventually tame an alien and hostile world.

Thoth of Hermopolis is the one who can teach us these lessons. We have already met him in his aspect of the sedate and stately ibis, which feeds in shallow waters, flies in V-formations, nests in flooded woodlands or on islands (such as Khebit), but we have not yet seen him in his other aspect as the baboon.

It is the latter, sometimes known as the Ape of Thoth, which will take us a little closer to Khemnu's spirit.

★

One of the few surviving pieces from the ruins of Hermopolis was a statue depicting a priest with a baboon on his shoulders. When such pieces do manage to survive the millenia we can be sure that they contain messages for us today. The statue itself was mightily battered, worn, but the drawing of it came through with a strange and peculiar detail, as though the original spirit behind the sculptor were saying: 'Remember this if nothing else remember this...

It was once a piece of European folklore that such apes were carried on the shoulders of fools and simpletons, perhaps in a distant memory of that city where such a thing was seen as a matter of course. Yet there has always an underlying notion that great wisdom can be expressed by 'playing the fool' in certain circumstances. It is well known that the word 'silly' is derived from *seely*, meaning happy, blessed, or even holy.

To some of the stuffier members of the Egyptian priesthood (and the gods know there were enough of those!) the initiates of Khemnu were an exasperatingly 'silly' lot.

Baboons were, and are, known as 'the dog-faced monkeys'. They are the largest and most intelligent of the Old World monkeys. Notoriously savage if provoked, and extremely powerful out of all proportion to their size, young baboons when tamed can still grow up to make affectionate and trustworthy creatures. The wild baboons sacred to Egypt were a mischievous and restless breed in their natural state, however, travelling in packs of up to 300, keeping close to open country and usually having one big, powerful male as their leader who always fights his way to the overlordship of the tribe. These baboons eat anything, but their favourite food is the scorpion which is sacred to Isis, and closely related to Khebit.

All the qualities of fight-or-flight, and learn and learn fast, can be found within baboons, as well as the prankish, trickster aspects of Hermopolis as a whole. We can discern Khemnu in them either through the wild jape, or the dry *pince sans rire* jokes of Thoth.

And when we laugh until we are sore, we unconsciously hold that area of our body which corresponds with Khemnu.

★

But the baboon holds mysteries beyond simple laughter. The dog-face, the long, large canine teeth, the man-like qualities, all necessarily evoked to the symbolist cast of the Egyptian mind, the air of Anubis, who was also a scavenger, and who also (via his American incarnation as Coyote)

manifested humour of the most disconcerting kind - an often extremely black humour.

Not only that but Anubis was extremely closely related to Sothis, the dog-star, which was so closely tied up with Egyptian ideas as to their spiritual origins. Even the Nemyss worn by royalty and seen in most images of Anubis, can be found paralleled by the baboon's long mantle of hair which sometimes splendidly bore the colours of Egypt.

Just as the adrenal glands can often be responsible for virilising manifestations in the female, and sexual precocity in the pre-adolescent male, so can we clearly discern when the female baboon is in heat.

So the symbol and reality of the baboon necessarily triggered off concepts in the Egyptian initiates which grouped together the concepts of Sirius, sex, our human and animal natures, and now brings into the open the long-standing occult tradition that mankind should never have 'descended into matter' in the first place, but should have continued to exist among the neters. It was when elements of mankind's free spirit decided to 'descend' and became involved in the procreative processes of certain ape-like creatures that the 'Fall into Matter' took place.

Whether the Traveller accepts this as initiatic truth, a deep allegory, or just another of the Tall Tales from Hermopolis that all wayfarers get inflicted with, is a matter for his or her own taste. Although if they are wise they will become like the baboon momentarily, and swallow everything, and gain energy from it as they digest.

★

So Khemnu, via the impulses of the baboon but under the decorous eye of the ibis, was the centre for all those impulses and cults which we might now call Priapic. These were not concerned with fertility as such - that was the concern of Abydos and Thebes - but with the intensity of sensual, erotic, and animal experience, and the universal concept of the male and female, positive and negative, locked together in a necessary union as hinted at by the binaries of Nun/ Nunet, Amun/Amunet, etc. If the intensity of that union could be fully understood, and prolonged or else developed, then enormous energies can surge through.

In this respect the use of the Hare as a symbol for this particular region within the psyche becomes more apparent. Like the strange frog-gods, the hare with its massive hind legs can swim well, although its sole mode of locomotion is by hopping. It can outrun almost all of its predators not only by speed alone, but by its ability to come to a sudden stop, or turn at a sharp angle.

In some ways we can almost find the spirit of Zen here, for the sudden and unexpected stop and change of direction was a common teaching method in Hermopolis just as it was among the Zen masters.

Prolific breeders whose defensive methods are always expressed through flight, the bucks or jacks as the males are called, nevertheless fight with tooth and claw amongst their kind in order to have the does, often leaping high in their frenzy - hence the phrase 'mad as a March hare'.

There was also a particular game played by the we'ebs in Hermopolis which was called, in effect, 'Running down the Hare' the object being to actually do that.

The difficulty in catching a hare was not so much in its speed but in those sudden changes of direction. Whenever a hare is about to make such a turn, however, its ears go back, though not all the way back. At this moment the we'eb must simply fling himself down at 90° to the hare's line of flight. He actually has a fifty-fifty chance of being right and catching with relative ease. It is not a matter of rapid analyses, or long internal debates as to terrain or mood of animal, but just a blind and unthinking dive toward the earth. The we'ebs wore simple loin-cloths and nothing else. They often attracted small crowds. They learned very early on that it is sometimes necessary to respond instantly and unconsciously toward given stimulii. Our animal and instinctive responses to the world have just as much a chance of bringing us to life and to light and to love as the finer, 'higher' senses.

*

Apart from the ways they travel through their respective mediums of earth and water, there is another comparison to be made between the hare and the frog in the light of their reproductive processes. Both of them can and do produce large numbers of offspring with great frequency.

The huge male frogs of Egypt - 8-10 inches in body length - will stand guard over their tadpoles, their heads only just above the water, ready to fend off attack from herons, from Man, and in particular from snakes.

Frogs were probably the first land creatures to use vocal sounds in order to communicate, and the chief purpose of these sounds was to bring the sexes together for breeding. Male frogs had the most developed voice, and the frog's tongue as it captures living prey is a clear symbol of the power of sounds - hence the Thoth connections, in his role as Communicator. The primitive sounds which were uttered as part of a direct adrenaline-response to sudden situations, later developed into words and consciously modulated cries for help. Speech came before thought. The frog-gods within us have come a long way under Thoth's guidance.

★

We cannot consider these frog-gods without looking at the snake-goddesses however.

If the most striking feature of the frog was its limbs, and its slow-blinking eyelids, then the snake is almost the direct opposite in these respects. On the other hand they both have notable tongues. And if the frog would use its tongue to call to Life, then the cobra which symbolised Woman would spit out Death with the same.

Because the female snake can store sperm, she is able to produce offspring several times after a single mating, and the eggs from which the young are hatched link back to the 'cosmic egg' at the centre of Khemnu's fragmented cosmology.

The cobra too, was seen to have two 'eyes' upon its hood and credited with the power of transfixing creatures (such as the hare) with its ruthless, unblinking gaze.

All of these creatures - hare, frog and serpent - are linked with the peculiar atmospheres evoked by those practices now grouped together under the name of witchcraft. They are also connected with those primary senses concerned with our sheer survival:

frog	voice
snake	sight
hare	hearing
baboon	smell

As for touch, that is up to the ibis, to Thoth in his more developed mode. Without touch we could not 'feel' the world. We would not be able to walk, hold things, respond or be able to cope in any way. The physical touch of sex would be without pleasure, mystery, or even import. The emotional sense of being 'touched' by something would make the world a cold place. The mental concepts of minds and ideas touching and mutually stimulating would not exist, and leave us in a fog. The spiritual sense of being touched by something greater than ourselves would be unknown, and leave us rotting in an abyss.

It is in this sense that Thoth ensures we make and maintain

links with all of our animal and reptilian aspects, opening all the levels of our primitive responses, harkening right back to the mid-brain again, and its neglected knowledge. The deities of Khemnu may exist within the realms of Infinity, Invisibility, Inertness and Nothing (which can link with the serpent, hare, frog and baboon respectively) but from these primordial, pre-human origins comes the abilities that will enable us to survive within, and ultimately master, the world.

Understandably this is why Thoth is often thought of as being married to Maat: they ensure that the Balance of Nature is maintained, that Man's role toward the animal world is akin to that of the priest carrying the baboon: a support, a relationship built upon respect and joy, and mutual origins. Maat is Thoth's anima: Thoth is the animus of Maat.

Thoth also ensures that when the trickster, prankster aspect of Khemnu breaks through into human consciousness and behaviour, they are in accordance with the natural justice of things.

★

Nothing exists now of any plans as to how Hermopolis may have looked in its heyday. Even the techniques of reaching it on magical levels are entirely a matter of chance, and the Henu Boat can rarely take us into the city itself, the former being too consciously developed as a mental structure. Khemnu runs through our consciousness like the hare, travelling at great speed and apparently with the mad, leaping joy of the witches' dance.

We can create a ritual using four pairs of men and women arranged in the pattern given below, and assuming the ancient names; but the knowledge of what to do then, and how to create the 'Egg of Light' from which the Word is born, is entirely a matter for the frog-like, serpent-like responses of the group as it functions in its most primitive manner, though all the while bound by the watchful and encircling figure of Thoth.

Magic of this sort is instinctive, even if such instincts do become highly developed with use.

As for the individual, he or she can try to enter with Kha'm-uast by stepping through that same figure as though it were a door. They can visualise themself on the back of a hare and riding through it while intoning the actual name of Khemnu. They can assume the god-form of a priest and feel the weight of the baboon on their shoulders, eventually lifting it down to find that its face is strikingly like their own. But in general the spirit of Khemnu will come to them rather than vice-versa. As they go throughout their life they must

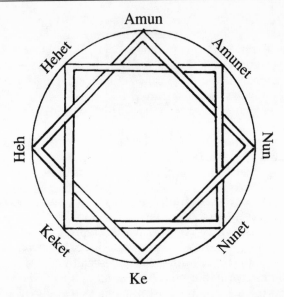

keep their eyes peeled, their ears open, their tongue silent but their nose twitching. At some moment, at some unpredictable and undefinable time, the wild and primitive spirit of the place will appear within their reach. All they have to do then is make a choice - any choice - and dive toward the earth to grasp it.

Or if they have the nerve they can take a large mirror and set it on their lap in a dark and empty room, sitting legs apart and frog naked with the reflection of the moon's light in the glass, and intoning Khemnu, Khemnu, Khemnu... with a frog-like croaking in the throat, and they will watch while their face changes through its other masks, other *ba* manifestations, back through the ages towards the source.

That, like Khemnu itself, is not for everyone. So every Traveller should look forward to the day when their own divinely inspired act of folly might appear to offer them the keys to the city.

If the fool who persists in his folly becomes wise, as William Blake once said, then he will come to Khemnu also.

ABYDOS

According to the esoteric tradition, Heaven's message was given at Heliopolis, repeated at Memphis, written in Thoth's writing and sent to Thebes, where Amon gave the reply that would kill or quicken. Really, it is an expression of the kabbalistic notion that the universe manifests itself through the descending levels of Emanation, Creation, Formation, and Action - although we should lose no sleep in trying to compare those systems too closely.

But the great problem in studying the spirit of Egypt at the remove of so many aeons, is that by concentrating so much on the esoteric and initiatic traditions, we can so easily lose touch with the common people. No matter how profound a religious concept or divine symbol may be, neither will last long at all unless they can touch the soul of the Common Man. The mystery traditions of Aunu, Men-nefer, Khemnu and Uast were all very wondrous, and linked to populist elements, but nowhere in Khem did the Common Man find as much delight as in Abtu, or Abydos to give it the present name.

With its largely public performances of the mysteries, Abtu was like Oberammagau, was like the medieval Glastonbury pilgrimages, was like the Mayday Parade, Saint Patrick's Day celebrations and every drunken meeting of the Young Farmers' Association at their annual ball, and all grouped around a single overwhelming truth: that a god died and was then reborn; and because of that, even the humblest soul in Egypt could attain an immortality of his own.

When we touch upon the spirit of Abtu we see the ordinary world as it groups around that simple, central belief. We glimpse the naked children who were shaven but for their single 'lock of youth', which the Sem retained as an allusion to the haunting truth that only by becoming like little children could we enter the realm of the neters. We glimpse the market places where vendors sold woven, wool-decorated carpets - 'magic carpets' they always insisted - right next to the numerous take-away stalls which sold lentil or onion soups, or any number of stews, all served out in simple, graven bowls of baked clay which only the foreigners failed to return, much as we now keep towels from an hotel. We see the amulet and trinket and jewellery and antique stalls, some of which operated an 'under the counter' black market in items which had been plundered from tombs. We smell the stalls of freshly-made bread, of which there were nearly 60 varieties, often made into animal shapes, and some of them quite obscene; and up-market stalls which sold ostrich plumes for the better quality tourist; and rows and rows of vegetable produce grown at home and getting cheaper as the day progressed, and large vats hauled in by donkey and cart in which fresh-killed meat was pickled...and we see the large, star-struck eyes of young lovers who would watch the sacred procession with its priests in jackal masks leading on before the sacred barques and the figures of the neters, and hear them whisper the same endless words: 'Ooh...it must have happened just like that in the olden days.'

Abydos is a parade, a celebration of the dreams of ordinary folk. Like Disneyworld it focussed around men and women wearing the masks of strange animals. Anyone too sophisticated or too stuffy to enjoy that sort of thing will never get far in Abydos.

★

Kha'm-uast actually chose this centre to build his 'monument for eternity', as they called it, in his case a deliberately flawed statue engraved with words and sentiments that we can use to summon, stir, and call him up. His grave was in Saqqara but his monument in Abydos was a psychological and magical link between the Lower and Upper Kingdoms. In building it there, however, he was only following the fashion of the time: families would have their loved ones' mummies transported to Abydos before returning for burial at home. It was not so much a case of 'See Abtu and die', but 'See Abtu regardless'. Other families whose aspirations could not quite match their resources, would include model boats in their tombs which could be used to transport them to that centre after death, in a clear echo of our present use of the Henu Boat. Memorial columns abounded like the nails on a fakir's bed.

Kings of the earliest Dynasties were buried here. Enough brick ruins have survived to indicate that preliminary versions of Djoser's Step Pyramid were experimented with. Yet beyond these, beyond anything or anyone else, the attraction for the common folk lay in their earnest belief that their beloved Osiris lay in Abtu. And if they could, by pilgrimage and devout acts and a bit of shopping in between, link with his spirit in some small way, then they too could live for ever, just as he does.

High or Low, Northern or Southern, Prince or Pauper... Osiris offered hope to everyone.

★

When we first approach Abtu on the inner planes, however, it is not Osiris whom we see. Taking the Henu Boat from Hermopolis and using the Nome Symbol as well as the name Abtu itself, what we actually glimpse as we head into the rays of setting sun is a long stretch of horizon with the sunlight splaying over it like the talons of a hawk, and what seems to be a vulture circling over a particular spot in the distance, beyond that line.

As we come closer two great shapes rise from the horizon, like the symbols for the planet Sirius. /\ /\

And then as the horizon falls we find them joined in what could almost be a crude symbol for the *ka*: /\/\

Nearer still, when the eyes and nose emerge from the desert waste beyond, we realise that we are looking at the colossal astral form of Khentamentiu, the jackal god who is 'Foremost of the Westerners' and 'Ruler of the Dead'.

At this point the Henu Boat's progress takes on a peculiar rhythm: rapidly forward and then slowly back a little way; rapidly forward more and slowly back. It is only when you get close enough to realise how vast the figure is that you recognise the Henu Boat as being involved in that god's breathing pattern - to such an extent that you will soon be sucked into its massive and opening mouth...

★

Intrepid travellers in magical realms will allow themselves to be consumed by this neter. It is a fate which all magicians experience at some time, one way or another. Like the baboons of Thoth, the jackals of Khentamentiu will eat anything, any offal, any dead flesh. That which is 'dead' or unproductive within us is always prime meat for Khentamentiu. He grinds, he chews, he breaks us up; and with those digestive processes regulated by the pancreas, he derives energy for the world's soul.

It is here at Abtu, in Khentamentiu's realm, that many of the complex and esoteric themes of previous ages, in previous centres, are broken down and used for the popular consumption. Without the peculiar qualities of Khentamentiu, the whole mass of Egyptian philosophy would be indigestible: it would stick in the throat; or else lie so heavily in the stomach that we would develop heartburn or worse.

★

Khentamentiu was the protective neter of Abtu from pre-dynastic times. According to his priests he was one of the oldest figures in the land - although as seasoned travellers by this time we can afford to smile at this oft-repeated claim. It is at Abtu that the neters of Khentamentiu, Osiris and Anubis play out their mysteries in a way that often overlaps to a bewildering degree.

Khentamentiu, in fact, became absorbed by the cult of Osiris to such an extent that the neter now became known as Osiris-Khentamentiu, which reflects the Egyptian habit of overlapping the developing theogonic concepts. That is, the old form of one neter is associated with or otherwise linked to the newer form to show the progression from one era to another. There is nothing particularly esoteric about his process: it is rather like an actor being compared with a similar type from a previous generation, and finds himself described as the 'new Valentino', or whatever.

But Khentamentiu was (and of course is) made of sterner stuff than mere celluloid, because Osiris never *quite* consumed him. And in the decades and centuries to come it will seem as if it were the older figure which triumphed in the god-eating stakes.

★

The term 'jackal' is actually a term of convenience, because there are elements of the fox and the loyal hunting dog in there also.

Khentamentiu is often directly associated with Anubis (or Anpu) but it is the jackal's couchant form of Wepwawet that holds the more direct link. Wepwawet, or Upuat, is more truly the inner aspect of Osiris himself, while Anubis is Osiris' son. Khentamentiu/Osiris/Anubis represent another Triple God image that might be (very loosely) described as grandfather/father/son - or the same energy in differing modes of expression at differing times.

The Traveller, however, should not let himself get too distracted in the effort to unravel such trinities. If they want to, the neters will explain themselves to him in their own way at a time when he best needs the knowledge. Which is not always the same as the time when he most wants it.

This black dog or dog-headed man is the conductor between levels of consciousness, the 'Walker Between the Worlds' who is equally at home in Hell as he is in Heaven. In one role he is Time itself, breaking all things down and yet ensuring that we will one day see their return, via the formula of 'plus ca change...'.

The exaggerated glottal sounds made by young children when they noisily gulp their food can be made to hint at Up-uat. All things are broken down within the digestive tracts of the Jackal.

Figure 19 - Anubis priest

*Figure 20 - Priest masked as Wepwawet during the
Mysteries of Osiris at Abydos*

Osiris, who is the true focus of the mysteries of this Black Dog, was originally the fetish of a dominant clan in the middle of the Delta region, and thus the mid-brain. As 'Lord of Djedu' he was the focus of a fertility cult - the earliest kind of religious upsurge known to mankind. He, and the kings who were identified as being his 'channel' to use a modern but occasionally accurate term, was credited with the power to influence or control Nature, thus making the land and the king One.

Although his original cult centre was at what the Greeks called Busiris, another one developed here at Abtu, or Abydos, where the 1st Dynasty tomb of Djer was found, but which was mis-read at the time as Khent. Hence the belief that Osiris himself was buried here. A further legend developed which stated that Isis found her husband's head here, and early worshippers thus hon-oured him by setting up corn heads on poles, adorned with wigs, feathers and horns - much like certain fetishistic practises of the European Celts. This was also expressed via the Nome symbol for the area, which was a bee-hive shaped structure surmounted by two feathers and decorated with a head-band and ureaus.

In the language of Khem, the words for honey and the spiritual essence (the *ba*) sounded similar enough to strike sparks of association.

A Lord of Crops, Osiris became omnivorous in the god-eating realm. He swallowed Andjeti, took great chunks from Khentamentiu, and swallowed certain choice aspects of Ptah and Sokar whole. But none of that mattered to the common folk who saw him in the simplest of terms: as a good man slain by his brother, who gained immortality through his loving wife. Osiris was hu-man, he suffered. Osiris was Everyman, who could also be found via the plants and animals upon which humanity depended.

In this respect it must be understood that there were only three seasons in Egypt:

Inundation - when the Nile flooded the land and deposited its silt, which made it fertile.

Going Forth - when the river returned to normal and the planting of crops began.

Deficiency - when the harvest occurred and the river was at its lowest.

The actual ceremonies of Osiris took place at the end of Inundation. When the Djed column was set in place by the Sem, it was a signal akin to the cry 'Christ is Risen', and meant that seeds could be planted for the new cycle.

★

Our knowledge of Osiris,whose true name is Asar, or User, is largely derived from two sources: the Pyramid Texts, as mentioned in the visit to Saqqara, and the countless inscriptions and reliefs on the walls of temples throughout Egypt; plus the Stela of Ikhernofret.

Ikhernofret was chief treasurer in the reign of Sesotris III who was sent to Abydos to reorganise and partially finance the developing cult of Osiris, as well as replenish and redecorate the temple.

Now the very oldest parts of Abydos consist of little more than a few stone door jambs and lintels which have survived long after the brick surrounds collapsed into the dust, as a symbol almost, that true gateways will always survive - somehow. The massive temples built in later Dynasties by Seti I and developed by Rameses II offer considerably more than just a few Gateways, but even these are less valuable than the words which Ikhernofret set down in a way that was meant to last for an eternity - and almost has.

★

Ikhernofret was to describe himself in the mysteries of Osiris with some pride:

> 'I played the 'Beloved Son' for Osiris-Khentamentiu. I built his large eternal boat. I created for him a sanctuary which elevates the beauty of Khentamentiu, of gold, silver, lapis lazuli, copper, sandalwood and ebony. I fashioned the gods of his following and renewed their shrines. I installed the priests and the hour priests in their tasks and gave them daily orders on the calendar feasts. I supervised the work on the neshemet barque and made its shrine. I decorated the god's breast with lapis lazuli and turquoise, gold, and all precious stones as protection for the divine members.'

The title 'Beloved Son' entailed the priest carrying out funeral cermonies for a superior, based upon the ideal divine son Horus who performed these rites for his father Osiris. Although Ikhernofret does not seem to have been a priest in the full sense of the term, he was clearly ritually qualified to carry out such a task. The barques mentioned are little portable carrying ships (first cousins to our own Henu Boat) which were mounted on platforms supported by poles and borne on the shoulders of the priests. The shrine boxes fitted into the barques contained the statuettes of the neters, and these were either solid gold or more usually gold-plated wood that was heavily adorned with jewels. The sacred drama of Osiris took place at other sites within Egypt but they assumed their greatest intensity here at Abtu where the earliest kings of Upper Egypt were buried, so the site's reputation as a portal between Heaven and Earth became established very early on. They considered that the Unseen came closest to being Seen at Abtu; Earth touched most directly upon Heaven here, and entry to the Beyond was entirely possible. Even today there is a discernible, numinous quality about what is otherwise a barren place and the feel that a person might step bodily through in certain circumstances if only they dare.

★

There were three phases to the ceremonies of Osiris:

1. The Departure of Wepwawet.
2. The Great Procession.
3. The Return to the Temple.

These were each related to the seasonal round and the rise and fall of the River Nile to such an extent that Osiris became identified with that too. In Abydos, among many other things, the circle of consciousness and the life-force of the individual with all its cycles of growth and decay and something-in-between, *was* Osiris. But beyond all else where there was Osiris, there was love; and where there was love Osiris could be found also.

Whenever we approach Abtu on magical levels we always arrive during the parade, which always seems to proceed from right to left as we view it in our vision, and always in the last hour before sunset.

Kha'm-uast invariably disappears into the crowd at this point. He has duties of his own to perform. The Traveller finds themself as one within the crowds from all over Egypt, edging forward to see the gods as they saw them.

Watch as the common folk jostle around; the men with their frizzed beards, dyed and plaited and set off to perfection with gold or silver threads which were all the rage in Kha'm-uast's time; mature women bright with make-up which invariably smudges at some inconvenient point and runs down the long white pleats of their linen dresses; young men discreetly carrying small pouches which contain the latest line of condoms made from the intestinal lining of sheep, or similar, their eyes more upon the free young women than the deities which are sweeping by; children on their parents' shoulders, carried with as much care as the priests carried the neters' statues, cold from the night air and wailing to go home as children, wearied Travellers, and wise men always do.

And then glimpse, in the last moments of daylight, the flaring of the torches, their long necklaces of light streaming away behind the Anubis priests who lead the procession, each one concentrating fiercely against the weight of the huge mask and shoulder-pieces, walking with a slight sway to the slow beating of drums. Then behind them the priestesses of Isis with their sistrums ready for every ninth beat, and behind *them* the priests carrying the portable barques which bear the shrines in which the sacred images ride. And then the neshemet barque itself, containing Osiris' body, larger and more splendid than the rest, the jewels catching the firelight and making everyone gasp at the way it seems to sparkle with its own luminescence. Then more torches and more priests and priest-esses assuming the roles of the appropriate neter, and then the Nome Standards of all Egypt, each one carried by the honoured representative.

Watch as the Anubis priests at the front of the snake literally and magically open the way through the crowds and the common consciousness, and hear the singers at the rear of the column bringing with them their strange songs from another world which were not so much concerned with words as the rising and falling of certain vowel sounds, and all the singers using hand-signals to direct the instrumentalists in a way that made them look as if they were weaving with light - which they really were.

And then, as the sun finally sets, glance northward to the low ridges beyond Abtu where a lone jackal, tempted by the priestly offerings, sits on a height and emits its dreadful cry, several times in succession, each call in a slightly higher key than the previous, giving its own raw version of the singers' lament before it shrinks back to its underground burrow to give its young ones a feast.

★

It is in Abtu that you can share sweat with the Common Man. Often you can pick up his or her concerns and be so startled by how similar these are to your own that the link can break.

In Abtu, in that procession which winds through the com-mon Egyptian consciousness like the great serpent which slithers through the worlds of Night, the common folk could see the living spirit of the neters with their own mortal eyes, and join in with those forces which ensured that the tides of life and love and all good things would function as they should.

★

The endocrine gland associated with Abydos is that of the pancreas, which lies in a narrow line across the posterior wall of the abdomen and consists, like the Procession, of several sections known as the head, neck, body and tail. While the head inclines downward, much as Wepwawet leads the procession into the Underworld, so the tail inclines upward, much like the crowds who 'tailed on' at the end of the parade hoping to touch heaven.

Pancreatic tissue consists of small lobules known as acini, which are filled with those cells which secrete the pancreatic juices containing the digestive enzymes. These play a vital part in the digestion of most foods: splitting fats and proteins, and converting starch into sugar, much as the spirit of Abtu turns the starchiness of esoteric religion into something sweet and pleasant for the common taste.

It is within these 'breaking down' processes that we can glimpse the Scavenger, as already mentioned. Jackals, for example, follow lions in order to finish off the carcasses, breaking them down just as Time devours all things. Like Time, too, scavengers such as Khentamentiu will eat almost anything, and transform it into an energy which is sufficient for its own needs.

The pancreatic juices are first cousins to the Jackal's drool. Osiris/Khentamentiu/Anubis are the true links between the worlds because it is pointless a man growing crops or keeping cattle if the food he produces cannot be broken down within him to produce energy: it would be pointless even trying to relate to the animal and vegetable worlds and join in with the cycle if there was no energy to be had from it, no life to result.

Wepwawet/Anubis/Khentamentiu - call him what you will - 'walks between' or otherwise links the worlds in more than the purely esoteric or occult senses.

★

Situated between the acini are numerous groupings of ductless cells known as the Islands of Langerhans, and these function as the endocrine glands proper, secreting insulin and glucagen into the bloodstream, which thus circulate through the body much as the *ab*, or heart, was held to circulate 'intelligence'.

Insulin and glucagen act opposingly, like serpents twining

~ 122 ~

around a staff; glucagen increases, while insulin decreases, the levels of sugar in the blood. Both are essential to maintain the balance of the carbohydrate metabolism. As with the levels of the River Nile, too much or too little can cause disasters either way.

And much the same can be said about spiritual energies also.

★

From the Temple of Osiris the procession invariably travelled to the mysterious and symbolic 'tomb' of Osiris, at a place called 'Peqer', or 'Poqer', which is near a range of barren hills in the desert. Changes are made by this time and Osiris is no longer in his neshemet barque but another, and he is addressed now as 'Unnefer', meaning variously 'Beneficent Being' or 'One who Defies the Decay of Death'. Another sense might well be that of 'Justified One'. One of the features of the whole procession is that it comes under ritual attack at two separate stages, one being at the 'shore of Nedyet', or 'The Murder Place', where Set and his cohorts slew the god Osiris. At each point the enemies are driven off, though not without ceremonial difficulty, by the Anubis priests in their roles as Guardians, which is one of Anpu's titles.

After the final attack the statue is returned to the tomb in the Temple of Osiris and the Sem-priest makes his appearance. At this point the public were excluded from the inner sanctum. They never witnessed what it was that the Sem did, but then they did not need to: for them, mystery alone was sufficient: mystery plus a warm bed and a loving partner.

But what happened within the sacred environs of Osiris' tomb was that the current Sem for Abydos would go into a trance, a 'temple sleep', before the statue of Osiris while enwrapped in a garment that made him strangely reminiscent of a bee.

In this role he was playing the 'Beloved Son' as Ikhernofret had done many years before, assuming the role of Horus to the statue's Osiris. In his dreaming, trance state, he would go looking for the soul of his father and catch it as one might catch a night bird, installing it into the statue which was now regarded as having a soul, and actually alive.

The 'Horus-sleep' could take all night, sometimes, depending upon the external circumstances of the nation. Sometimes, Osiris seemed very far from his countrymen indeed.

In the morning, still half-wrapped in the bee-stripes, he would watch while the Djed pillar was erected, announcing to a jubilant crowd that Asar-Un-nefer, the Green Man and Horned God, had triumphed over death once more.

After the cheers, a new statue of the neter was dedicated. A great public offering then followed to the neter's new image. All this took place within the outer courts of the temple. To the pilgrims this was the best moment of all: they linked arms, held hands, kissed and sang songs as people in the West would do when Auld Lang Syne announced that the Old Year was over and a New Year just beginning.

★

The last part of the ceremony which Kha'm-uast performed in his true role as Sem, was known as the 'Opening of the Mouth', referring to the moment when the Sem animates the statue by touching its mouth with an adze-like tool, or wand. Now considering the mass testimonies of countless sober Catholics that certain statues in their churches (usually of the Virgin) have been seen to move, or weep, and show signs of actual life, we would be fools to completely reject the notion that inanimate matter can suddenly become animate. There are obvious psychological factors involved here which may relate to hysteria, mass-suggestion or a collective hypnosis, all keyed-in and triggered off by the effects of lighting and mood, but we should not feel that the whole experience has been thus 'explained'. Soaring emotion and spiritual kinds of ecstacy can have a life-long and transforming effect whether they are caused by pure miracle or pure suggestion.

Insofar as we can provide a rationale to the 'Opening of the Mouth' ceremony or indeed any ceremony which affects consciousness, it is perhaps more likely to be found within the methods of talismanic magic than in any other occult discipline.

In this, the magician takes an object, links it by symbols and symbolic acts which touch chords deep within him (which also echo high spiritual principles) and uses this as a focus. The object - the talisman - is a means of expressing dynamic energies as these are expressed both within the realms of the gods and also within the magician's subconscious.

This is the scheme of the neters again: a peculiar type of energy expressing itself in similar ways through all the worlds of manifestation. Kha'm-uast animating the statue of Osiris was charging a talisman that would influence not just him, but the whole of the nation. It was alive for the common folk if no one else: god made manifest in stone. The Sem, as the focus for the consciousness of the people as a whole, would work changes within his own psyche and also the psyches of his followers.

This was the true purpose of the Sem. In previous ages and even today, it was also the role of the Shaman.

Despite the complexity of worship in Khem, and the extraordinarily developed theocracies, striking parallels with shamanism can be glimpsed throughout the whole culture. It is not shamanism in its pure and simple form wherein a man or woman would act as a link between the tribe, its ancestors and animal spirits, and the actual area in which they lived, but it is shamanistic in its broadest sense.

The sketch in Figure 7b was made in the Archaic Period, circa 5000 to 3000 BCE, which seems to indicate a masked man with pipes. This, taken from the back of the Oxford Palette, could have been lifted straight from one of the cave walls in the Ariege, where humans were once drawn wearing the guise of stags. This may well be the ancestor of all those priests and priestesses in Egyptian temples who donned the masks of animals in order to invoke the neters - not simply within themselves, but in the hearts of those who watched, and kept the faith. There are elements here of both Set, in his secret role as Lord of the Dance, and Anubis too, who was actually far closer to the husband of his mother than to his own father, Osiris. Between them, in fact, they are leading a procession of their own that will take humanity into the next aeon, if we learn how to follow them.

The primitive forms of shamanism developed in Egypt as it did throughout the world, but at the beginning of the dynastic period it streamlined itself into the cult of the Pharaoh, who was seen as a very powerful, divinely endowed shaman. Instead of being linked to a small tribe in a small area with a local totem, the spirit of Pharaoh covered all of Khem, which now had two totem creatures which took precedence above the rest: the Vulture for Upper and the Cobra for Lower Egypt. While at intervals throughout his reign the Pharaoh would hold the Heb-Sed festival in which he made a ritual progress through the neters via the standards of all the Nomes, like a shaman between totem poles, symbolically asserting his fitness to be the supreme link between them all, and the prime living focus between the people, the land, and their deities.

Memories and remnants of the archaic shamanism lingered over into dynastic times, as witnessed by such things as we have glimpsed in Abtu: the Sleeping Sem, the Calling of the God which was tied to the fertility of the land and the people; the symbolic 'qenau' garment which is called the 'coat of protection', which parallels the ritual clothing that the shaman would wear on his journey to, or contact with, the Otherworld; the skins and feathers and headpieces...

Within the religious myth, too, Osiris' body was dismembered and scattered; Isis had to search out each part and reassemble him with Thoth's help; while in contemporary shamanism the aspirant has to undergo a ritual death wherein the person's body is dismembered or otherwise taken apart and reassembled in some magical and/or psychological way - the process of which confers shamanistic powers.

And just as animals play a major part in shamanism by acting as spirit guides, familiars and totems, so can the intense Egyptian respect for animals and magical use of animal imagery take on a new meaning when looked at with a shaman's eye.

Indeed, Osiris is constantly depicted, via his atef crown, as being a Horned God, like the tutelary deities of almost all shamanic and witch cults of the world. The challenges and ritual sacrifices, the feasts (often consuming the dead king) all find clear echoes within those ritual practices derived from the Osirian Cycle. In this respect it is Anubis (who was the ritual assassin of the pharaoh and/or devourer of the Apis Bull) who shows us the most direct links between the seemingly impenetrable complexities of Khem and the similar Cults of the Sacred King throughout Europe. The jackal-god hints at the Horned God via his upright ears, while his name Wepwawet was written

While the symbol ⩔ means simply the head, or foremost part of anything, it necessarily triggers off associations between himself, the Apis Bull, and the Horned God of Osiris whose inner aspect he really was.

If Abydos is to teach us anything, it is that magic can never be for ourselves alone, but for the common folk with whom we belong. If the Traveller ever yearns to become a Sem, they must learn the lessons of the shaman first. These are gut lessons, all of them.

★

In architectural terms many kings have left their mark within Abydos, but none more so than Seti I and Rameses II.

The temple of Seti I was built to an unusual L-shaped plan (see Figure 22) with two pylons through which the sun-god entered at noon, two courts and pillared porticoes, followed by two hypostyle halls and then seven adjacent sanctuaries dedicated to Seti I, Ptah, Ra-horakhty, Amon-Ra, Osiris, Isis and Horus, behind which were shrines to the last three plus a mysterious room of two square columns that was designed to be completely inaccessible. There were chapels also for the Memphite gods of Ptah, Sekhmet and

Nefertum, plus enough hieroglyphic symbolism to give the story of all Egypt if they could be read properly, and one of the earliest king lists known,which helped to give a semi-mythological history to the land. There was also a wondrous relief of Seti I and Rameses II lassoing a bull while Wepwawet looks on - which is almost a formula for what has been discussed about Abydos. The inner reliefs were generally done under the direction of Seti I; the outer were commissioned by his son Rameses II.

Behind the temple itself was the Oseirion, the fabled tomb of Osiris himself, as they thought. This was approached from the north through a long, sloping corridor down which elements of the Procession would surely have gone, entering what was essentially an artificial mound which aped the Primeval Mound of Atum. This was formed by huge square pillars of red Aswan granite which supported massive architraves of similar. In the centre of this hall (which was not entirely covered from the sky) was a small raised platform with steps on two opposing sides, and which was once surrounded by water in an echo of Nun.

Although Seti's temple is remarkably well-preserved today, the Oseirion is a ruin, but an intensely evocative one for all that.

Of all the places in Abydos, no Traveller should miss going there. Even Osiris had to go back to his source at intervals in order to recharge, much like exiled patriots return home at intervals in order to refresh themselves.

★

We can easily construct the image of the Oseirion and enter it with Kha'm-uast via the long descending corridor. The method is no different to that used in working with other scenes already described. By this time the Traveller will have some notions of their own as to how to do this, and why, and needs no literary hand-holding now.

One very simple technique which will get us closer to the spirit of Osiris in a different way, however, does not involve building up images within the creative imagination so much as breaking them down. It involves simply lying on your back in your garden, or in your local park, or even in your bed at night, and beginning the Sleep of Osiris. The ideal stipulation is that this place should be where you feel a sense of belonging - your actual home, or your home territory, or somewhere that evokes the qualities of your *ideal* home.

Assume the position of Osiris as you lie. Build up the god-form. Feel the weight of the atef crown on your head. At this point imagine that your surroundings are dissolving...all the walls, all the houses, all the trappings of the modern world, until you can visualise yourself as lying in the open on the surface of a world that has not yet been touched by man.

Feel the solidity of the earth under your backbone. Have a sense of your vertebrae linked together like djed columns. Then imagine yourself sinking into the ground and indeed falling through the surface as Lucifer must have fallen down through the skies. Feel yourself tumbling over and over, down through the geological layers, through denser and denser matter to the very heart of the earth as it lies directly below your normal home, while gently intoning *Asar, Asar, Asar* with *Aset, Aset, Aset* as a mental undertone.

Women Travellers can perform this technique as effectively as men, more so in fact. They can either forget about the god-form aspect entirely, or regard themselves as Osiris' anima, or assume the form of either Isis (Aset) or Hathor, or whichever goddess feels most appropriate for this stage of the Journey.

At some point the Traveller will come to the very heart of the Earth as it lies directly under your normal home. What he or she actually finds here is necessarily an individual thing: some find great caverns, some find an immense jewel-like core in which they can 'see' things, but more usually they might plunge into a brilliant molten core, which is like entering the dark sun in the heart of the night. Once consumed by this, as coarse bodies burn away, only the *ba* remains.

In the latter case the Traveller's mortal persona is consumed by the earth's inner fire as the body of the Divine King was once eaten by his worshippers. At this point an inner contact of varying intensity can be made with these subterranean or 'inner earth' beings which relate to your own particular area of concern - in both the geographical and the psychical sense. At very least your 'fall through matter' will have caused a channel to be broken open between the surface of your world and its internal energies, up which your own internal energies will now pour. This is when the Earth God or Goddess (who is yourself) becomes what Dylan Thomas described as 'The force that through the green fuse drives the flower'.

In time, when the images weaken or fade, rise to the surface again by an act of will until your consciousness springs from the earth back into your body like a new-born soul. But before you let the modern world reassemble itself, look once more upon the greenery around and feel yourself a part of it in all its cycles and wondrous fertility.

Even if you live in the most dreadful concrete wasteland,

then there will still be ways and levels through which you Osiris-Traveller will bring lushness, growth and energy of an appropriate sort into the world.

This is one of the first steps along the shaman-path. It is one of the first steps to becoming a Sem.

★

By this time the Traveller may have noticed that Kha'm-uast is not quite so prominent on the Journey as before. In fact he has no intention of going any further than Abydos. If the Traveller has not, by this time, gained some slight insight into how to conduct the rest of the Journey alone, making their own links between the outer and the inner, then they probably never will. If the Traveller does not want, at some stage, to become his or her own guide, their own 'walker between the worlds' and sole master of the Henu Boat then they are never likely to gain access to the true spirit of any Journey. So whether we like it or not, Abydos is where our guide takes his leave, and we become initiated Travellers who will go on, by ourselves, or return with good grace. Either way, this is the place where the guide demands his fee...

★

At some point during his many historical visits to Abydos, either as Sem-priest for the mysteries or simply as overseer to his father's massive programme of building work, Kha'm-uast had his 'Monument for Eternity' built, although this could equally be translated as 'Image for Eternity'.

Despite the splendid title this is a simple enough piece, a statue of himself which can be seen today in the British Museum, wonderfully carved from some deliberately chosen, flawed material which seems to proclaim that despite his legendary status he really was human underneath it all, with just as many rough and unworkable edges as any of us. As Crown Prince he could have chosen something colossal to leave behind: his father was never hesitant about doing that. Yet he prepared himself a piece which could fit into any living room, and which he knew, perhaps, would be easily transportable from his native land.

Some psychics insist that the statue overflows with magnetism. Others who are no less sensitive can feel little or nothing at all. Either way it can still speak to us across the millenia. If we listen to the inscriptions on this one statue we will hear the words of a hierophant speaking across time, not only to his neters but to us. The payment he demands as guide is thus a simple one: that one day, in a quiet place, we will build up his image via any of the illustrations given so far and read his words out loud. Whether we understand them or not is of supreme indifference to him. He knows, as do all Initiates and seasoned Travellers, that meanings will impinge upon us in their own time, in differing ways.

By saying his words out loud we are, in a sense, doing towards his 'Image for Eternity' what he once did for the statue of Osiris during his temple sleep. We are 'Opening the Mouth' in a way that will enable the ancient deities of a half-remembered land to find their voice and influence again.

★

Kha'm-uast begins by inscribing his monument for eternity with the names and titles of his father, Rameses:

'The Good God, Lord of the Two Lands, User-maat-Ra-setep-en-Ra, beloved of the Two Enneads which are in Abydos.

Son of Ra, Lord of Diadems, Ramessu-mery-Amon, beloved of Osiris, Chief of the West.'

Then he addresses himself to the 'First Cause' as it was determined in the Mystery Teachings of Aunu:

'O Atum, may you give breath to the King's Son and Sem-Priest Kha'm-uast, this sweet breath which is in your nostrils! The King's Son Kha'm-uast, justified, takes his seat upon this great throne which is in Hermopolis. The King's Son Kha'm-uast guards the egg of the Great Cackler; as it is firm, so is the King's Son Kha'm-uast firm; as it lives, so he lives, and as it breathes the air, so he breathes the air.'

Next Kha'm-uast states what he himself has caused to have done, and the reason for doing it. He explains why he has had the statue made and why it was placed where it was in Abydos, or Ta-wer:

'The King's Son Kha'm-uast, he made it as his monument, his statue for millions of years, to exist in Ta-wer for ever over the circle of the Lord of Eternity, a glorious place for invocation-offerings, the great place of the land of truth, the holy district of giving praise to the excellent beings that it may open its road to this excellent spirit who rests on the place wherein is the statue of the King's Eldest Son, beloved of him, the Sem-Priest Kha'm-uast.'

After this he addresses himself to the Lord of Ta-wer himself, who is of course Osiris:

'O Osiris, greatest of gods, more glorious than he who made him, may you behold that which the King's Son and Sem-Priest Kha'm-uast does. He has caused you to become great of form, he lives through you, O god, and you live through him. May you appoint him as your sole chamberlain! He is a protector who goes about the Necropolis, one who knows the road of passing. He has raised up [the Djed] he has protected Nkh, he has strengthened Him-Who-Sleepeth Upon-The-Thigh, he has confirmed Ii and Snh, he has protected mysteries. He opens the mouth of Sokaris himself; he has created magic in the womb of Nu, he opens the Royal Placenta, he has caused your throat to breath, he is one who grabs the arms of your enemies every day. May you appear gloriously in him as Lord of Ta-wer according as you give unto him life, stability, well-being and duration in your temple, for he is your son and champion.'

Figure 21 - Sphinx of the Divine Consort Shepenwepet II,
from Karnak, circa 665 BCE

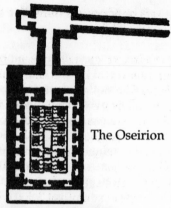

The Oseirion

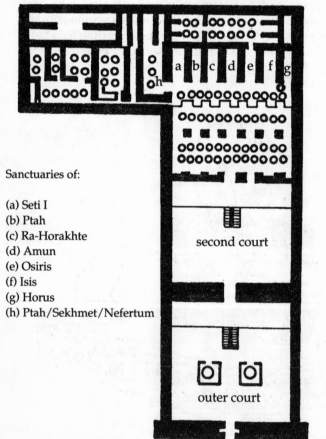

Sanctuaries of:

(a) Seti I
(b) Ptah
(c) Ra-Horakhte
(d) Amun
(e) Osiris
(f) Isis
(g) Horus
(h) Ptah/Sekhmet/Nefertum

second court

outer court

Figure 22 - Temple of Seti I, Abydos

Nkn, pronounced *Neken*, is an epithet for Osiris when he was injured. Kha'm-uast is here proclaiming himself as Osiris' Guardian. Ii and Snh, pronounced *Iy* and *Seneh* refer to Horus and Set respectively. 'Confirming Ii and Snh' is a reference to his ability to determine or judge the outcome of events when cosmic forces such as Horus and Set contend. Opening the mouth of Sokaris is a clear reference to his ability to conquer death itself, on magical levels, and enter the realms of dead at will. 'Creating magic in the womb of Nu' is his way of saying that he knows how, where and when his essence will manifest itself through reincarnation.

He ends his inscription on his monument for eternity with a response from the 'Divine Soul, rendered through the 'voice' of Osiris:

> 'An offering which Osiris, Chief of the West, gives...whom his mother's womb created in peace and triumph, glorious in Heaven and powerful in Earth, Chief Carpenter in the protection of his Lord; he who is at the head of the chisel, who opens the great road of Ta-wer so that he may rest upon its place at every festival...the Hall of the Two Truths on the day of reckoning the dignities of the King's Son, the...Sem-Priest who acts as the Pillar-of-his-mother, Kha'm-uast.'

We do not need to understand it with our conscious minds. Just reading it aloud, and with respect, will be payment enough for Kha'm-uast's services as guide.

Kha'm-uast, the Keeper of the Secrets of Heaven and Earth and the Duat, who knows the Necropolis and the Temple, who was a persistent Traveller himself on all planes of existence, who eternally renews himself through cycle after cycle, will be well pleased that the words he so carefully chose for his Image to Eternity have proved it to be exactly that, and have lasted for over three thousand years.

All we need do now on magical levels of visualisation is to take the *uas* wand we can see him offering us, energise our Henu Boat for the final stage of the present Journey and make our way to Thebes in the full knowledge that we are making channels in our psyche which will enable the best of the wonders of Egypt to set down patterns for the world's future.

THEBES

When Egypt entered its puberty, Thebes appeared. Thebes, whose original name was Wo'os, Wast, Uast or simply Uas, according to preference, was the place of the Sceptre, or the place of the ⸕ .

In the earliest days it was no more than a small town where Montu was worshipped, a pre-dynastic neter whose symbol was the bull. The bull, to the Egyptian mind, was a symbol synonymous with the *ka*. From being this small town, Thebes rapidly put on weight, and muscle, and grew out of all recognition, as young bodies always do at puberty. Our former guide Kha'm-uast, whose name means 'Manifestation in Thebes', would have seen the link between the *uas* wand and the bull-powers immediately.

Even today, as if echoing the overwhelming fascination that sex and sexuality seems to have for the masses, and the way it creeps into all aspects of everyday life whether we want it or not, Thebes contains more than three-quarters of all the Ancient Egyptian remains. The old gods assail from every side and at every opportunity; Theban power is flaunted; its imagery is omnipresent. A Traveller could lose his innocence in Thebes.

On the East bank of the River Nile there is the Great Temple of Amon, the Temple of Mut (his consort), and the Temple of the Infant Khonsu, who completes the trinity. All of these are to be found within that complex known as Karnak. A few kilometres to the South, joining these by an avenue of ram-headed sphinxes, is the great Temple of Luxor, which was known as the 'southern harem of Amon' where his human concubines could be found. On the West bank - as ever - was the place of the dead: the Valley of the Tombs of the Kings, where Tutankhamun, Ay, Horemheb and numerous Nobles were interred with the usual splendour, plus the royal mortuary temples of Merenptah (who succeeded Rameses II), Thutmose III and IV. There is the almost futuristic temple of Hatshepsut which actually inspired much 20th Century architecture, plus the Valley of the Tombs of the Queens, plus numerous temples and edifices to other individuals great and small. They all cluster together at either side of the Nile like the vesicles in the testes, and they can all conspire to create life.

All things poured down into Thebes. And when the royal courts left Memphis at the time when the Egyptian psyche was 'coming of age', Thebes was the obvious choice. Only later (*much* later) when Theban power began to over-reach itself, did the royal courts retire to that area in the Delta where we once looked for Khebit. That is another story however, and another aspect of endocrine functioning.

By the time of the 18th Dynasty Thebes had confirmed itself as the capital of all Egypt with a power that far eclipsed that of Memphis. It had the biggest and most splendid temples, attracted vast revenues, and inspired some of the greatest tombs in the land, filled with the greatest wealth. Thebes became known throughout the world simply as The City, as an expression of its uniqueness and dominance. Like adolescent youths and young adults generally, Thebans knew everything, and spoke as if they had invented sex and all the gods. At their worst, Thebans were insufferable.

★

At no time in ancient history did any area so solid, so substantial, derive from so insubstantial an energy as that of Amun. Amun had no *ren* as such. The hieroglyph simply meant The Hidden One, concealed as our sexual organs are concealed in adulthood, in public at least. The Hidden One, or the Invisible One, came down to Thebes from Hermopolis when his time had arrived. Despite the insubstantiality of Amun and his company, no other place in Khem contained such a treasure house of imagery as the temples and tombs dedicated to them. In Thebes, a Traveller can find power in its absolute sense, with all the corruption and cruelty and dissonance that power incurs when it is wielded rashly.

★

There is an overwhelming air of self-creation at Thebes, which veers toward the concept of parthenogenesis at times. More than anywhere else in Khem, Thebes is the place that we can give birth to ourselves, to use an accurate if hackneyed phrase. Thebes is where our initiation is completed and yet begins. It is the place where Man can touch the Woman within him, and where Woman can find her masculine aspects - just as Hatshepsut once assumed full pharaonic powers even to the extent of referring to herself as 'he', and wearing the symbolic beard. Thebes is the place where we can sniff the 'blood royal' within us, and learn the powers of the Royal Placenta.

★

This air of self-creation (which brings with it the themes of personal responsibility for all our actions) can be glimpsed in that Vulture Goddess known as Mut, who was believed to be capable of impregnating herself by opening her body to the wind. Amun, meanwhile, is seen in his aspect as Amun-Min, an ithyphallic figure who strives to the heavens as Geb was seen to do in Aunu; and then there is Khonsu, their wonderchild, who is usually seen in bindings so tight that his limbs cannot be differentiated, just like the undeveloped embyro in the earliest stages of pregnancy. We will return to all of these themes later.

In the drawing of the microcosmic man, Thebes is at the Sphere of the Moon, known to the kabbalists as Yesod, or Foundation. In that glyph the Moon is seen as the receptacle of all the divine energies pouring earthward - a grail of sorts in which all is contained and mixed, and from which all can be poured. It is also the sphere of the Muladhara and Svadisthana chakras, and those endocrine glands that are concerned with sexual reproduction, and the mysteries of the womb and woman. Thebes, via the reproductive processes, is that which supports the continuance of life. Without Thebes we would have no future. Thebes really is the foundation.

★

Many if not all of the themes and stages of the journey so far will find expression if not resolution within The City, just as many of the previous endocrine glands exert direct influences upon the ovaries or the testes of the individuals concerned. Often it is hard to tell whether things end up in Thebes or in fact have their truest origins there. Just as some people see sex everywhere they look, others can find Theban influences. Freud was born in Thebes, in the purely psychological sense.

Thus we can find clear traces of Ptah within both Amun and his son Khonsu, who shares similar mummiform wrappings. Mut, when she wears her more popular cat's head, is almost identical with Sekhmet. Whether this is

Khonsu

due to priestly aggrandisement or something more esoteric is not really important. On more levels than one we can find most of Egypt within Uast.

★

We can enter Thebes in the simplest of ways by standing in the prow of the Henu Boat and using the *uas* wand by ourselves for the first time to trace the image of the ankh in the air before us.

The ankh is often described as a stylised symbol of the vagina, but while there is necessarily truth in this of the symbolist sort, the ankh, or cross of life, is more truly an image of the uterus, the fallopian tubes, and the birth canal. The *uas* wand is, in itself, the actual Nome Symbol for Thebes, and simply by holding it with intent we can take the Henu Boat to any of the majestic sites on either side of the Nile. Visiting Thebes for the first time is like the wonder each teenager feels when visiting their nation's capital for the first time alone, and with a pocketful of money; it can overwhelm. Uas, as is the way with cities (and sceptres of power) can come alive and take over. Whether the individual can cope depends entirely upon the quality of his or her own *uas* powers.

Being wise, therefore, there is really only one safe place from which to approach Thebes for the first time: one place personal enough, interested enough, and central enough to allow each Traveller to get their bearings and also understand something of the city's spirit.

So as we stand at the prow of the Henu Boat and soar into the ankh, we must cry out the name *Isheru* as clearly as we can, and hope for a happy landing in the holy precinct surrounding the Temple of Mut at Karnak.

★

When we travel through (and also with) the neters to explore what is essentially the reproductive centre of Khem, we will always find ourselves at the place of the waters within the Precinct of Mut.

The sacred lake within the precinct curves around the actual Temple of Mut like a developing embryo in the earliest stages of pregnancy. The actual temple faces North, which is not usual, and hints at the magical belief that it is from the North, or place of darkness, that old souls can impinge upon the consciousness. More relevantly, it faces toward the Precinct of Amun to which it is joined by an avenue of ram-headed sphinxes, down which the god himself

~ 137 ~

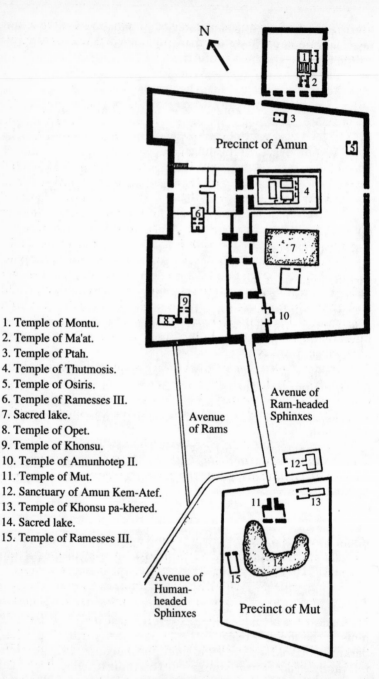

N

Precinct of Amun

1. Temple of Montu.
2. Temple of Ma'at.
3. Temple of Ptah.
4. Temple of Thutmosis.
5. Temple of Osiris.
6. Temple of Ramesses III.
7. Sacred lake.
8. Temple of Opet.
9. Temple of Khonsu.
10. Temple of Amunhotep II.
11. Temple of Mut.
12. Sanctuary of Amun Kem-Atef.
13. Temple of Khonsu pa-khered.
14. Sacred lake.
15. Temple of Ramesses III.

Avenue of Ram-headed Sphinxes

Avenue of Rams

Avenue of Human-headed Sphinxes

Precinct of Mut

Figure 23 - Karnak

attended by his priests and priestesses, and focussed in his statue, would come at intervals to mate with his wife. The sphinxes themselves refer to the Age of Aries (circa 1900 BCE) when the Ram of Amun began to dominate. When the noon sun reflected off the waters of the sacred lake, Mut in her temple was bathed in light, and she became as radiant as any woman in the first glow of a hoped-for pregnancy.

When we arrive at the lake shore we are no more than the small shadow of a hawk, nesting in one of the branches of the many shady trees that were grown there. From here we can see the priestesses abluting themselves, standing naked on the various levels at the lake's edge, washing as slowly and purposely as old folk in China practise their tai-chi. Dream-like and enrapt, they wash as much with light as they do with the water itself, in a way that our modern world has almost forgotten.

Whatever they may be like in their moments of power, during the magico-religious ceremonies attending their goddess, the priestesses *en masse* were never at all like the popular (invariably masculine) conception: infinitely serene, self-contained, sensual, wrapped within their mysteries. As a group they were like any collection of hard-working women anywhere, of any class: capable of outrageous and often vulgar humour when a lone male came into their sights. Young and virginal male we'ebs would dread being sent from the Precinct of Amun down to that of Mut on errands, for they would invariably meet with the raucous cries of 'Come on then sonny, where's your Hidden One then?' usually followed by 'Ooh I bet its Invisible!'. Men on building sites today could not demonstrate any behaviour, or call out any rude comments that did not echo those made by the Priestesses of Mut aeons before.

This is not poking fun at the spirit of Khem. The priests and priestesses were human after all, and not spiritual automata. We do them a disservice by visualising them as white-robed beings who were far removed from mortal concerns. By glimpsing the universal aspects of the modern world in Khem, we can set about making the best of that land come alive within us today.

The people of Thebes were human, all too human. They link with us via the generations of breeding that lie between.

★

At regular intervals, on sacred occasions, the priestesses (functioning in a purely professional way as the ceremony demands) would bring out the statues of their neters to wash within the lake. Linked as these were with the innermost response of each priestess, they would thus purify themselves and ultimately their whole sex.

This was not a rite exclusive to the Precinct of Mut, however, as Sacred Lakes were feature of most Egyptian temples, and Travellers should find their own. That in the precinct of Amun, for example, was a square, serious and masculine affair, 250 by 400 feet, and varying in depth from 8 to 12 feet. It was from such places that later notions of baptism developed in later religions.

Each Traveller will eventually find his own place of waters either within Khem or within the outer world of his own habitat. At such places we can cleanse and heal ourselves. We can learn to forgive ourselves also, as all Travellers must strive to do sometime.

At some point in this reverie on the shores of the Sacred Lake, we will necessarily meet the Lady. Places such as this (in all cultures) invariably have guardians attached to them. Some of them are pure and animal thought-forms, ensouled with enough force to create terrors in the mind of the unwelcome; some of them are decaying shells of once-human entities; some of them are formidable figures indeed and not so easily analysed.

The Lady Tui, to give her a name, was actually a Theban priestess from the 18th Dynasty. Tui has seen it all before, is totally unimpressed by any Traveller, and is only concerned that each one enters the Precinct with respect, and leaves it without a mark. Tui will act as our guide, well enough, for our short stay within the Precinct, but she makes it quite clear that she finds us all a little boring. As a mature woman in the perpetual prime of her power, there are other things she would rather be doing. Sometimes we can get the disconcerting feeling that she's laughing at us.

★

Tui invariably beckons us to the Temple of Mut proper, which was built by Amenophis III in the middle of the 18th Dynasty. We curve past the temple of Rameses III, which Tui seems to regard as never more than an impertinence, and around to the courtyard at the front, which is flanked with a circle of black granite statues dedicated to Sekhmet.

The name and key to the sanctuary itself is *Isheru*, the hieroglyphs of which contain a recumbent lion. We can build up a 'feel' of that circle of black granite goddesses and their lion heads - the solidity, the darkness and endurability, the power...we can hold the *uas* wand as our passport and right to visit, and we can ask permission from Tui, and hope that Mut will come from her temple and link with us via the wand, hand over hand, and tell us about the neters to which she belongs and the way that these were used by the

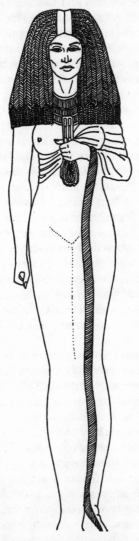

Figure 24 - Lady Tui

priestesses of Thebes to claim for themselves a power that is almost unimaginable.

It is in Thebes that we finally learn where Amun, the Hidden One actually hides himself. Amun, the Hidden One, hides within the power of Woman.

★

There was an experience that all priestesses in the Precinct of Mut underwent at certain times linked to the moon and their own natural cycles. As in any such enclave where women work together in either the ancient or modern world, the priestesses invariably menstruated at the same time. This was when the we'ebs (which was actually a title as applicable to the female as the male) would line themselves at the time of the full moon along the sides of the sacred lake, looking across toward the orb and its light upon the water.

The revelation that was induced in each one had nothing to do with any visionary jaunts or mystical levels of consciousness. It was based upon the simple observation that each priestess would see the moon's light shining in a narrow path across the water directly to her feet and hers alone, followed by the understanding that each individual was having the same perception. In other words, if they could have shared their visions, mingled them, then the whole lake and indeed the whole world would be seen as covered in a vast sheet of light. It is only the separate and lonely gaze of the 'unconnected' individual who insists upon the exclusive nature of that vision of the 'narrow path'. The narrow, silver light of the moon upon water links us all like an umbilical cord. It is only the mind which makes us separate; only the heart which can unite us all.

This in essence is the Vision of Mut, whose very name is the same root as the Egyptian word for mother. Mut is also Sekhmet and Isis and Nu and Neith and Hathor - and all the great goddesses who have ever borne a child for love, or else given birth to some great impulse for the sake of her fellow souls.

We can invoke her easily enough - more easily than any other neter for we are bound to her for eternities. We only need the moon and a stretch of water between, keyed-in by the appropriate meditations on the nature of the Mother, and she will come to us if we call: a slim lady in a blue dress which is patterned with feathers, the vulture head-dress made so cleverly that the bird's wings seem to be her natural hair, and the vulture's head like the traditional uraeus. In her right hand she will hold the ankh; in her left, the lily sceptre of Upper Egypt. You travel to meet each other along that line of light which binds you. When you meet, when you link and blend, that slim and narrow image reveals itself as enveloping the whole of life itself. Whatever anxieties and antagonisms you may have toward your own mother which you feel are holding you back, can be resolved via such a link with Mut.

It is never easy though: mothers, vultures and lionesses never are.

The Theban Triad contained Mut, Amon and Khonsu, as already mentioned. They were known universally as the Moon gods, if for no other reason than that they reflected the light and qualities of almost all the other neters in Khem. (And the Ancient Egyptians were well aware that the Moon is the reflector of the sun's light).

Here in the Precinct of Mut, beside that Sacred Lake which is forever pregnant with possibilities, we must learn about them all and also how to draw nourishment through that cord of light.

★

Like the malleable levels of the astral light, which are also the impressionable levels of the subconscious, Amun could take on any form, assume the features of any god. Like Jehovah, with whom he shared many common features, he began his career as an obscure deity who was worshipped in one small semi-desert locale and eventually became the supreme god. Like Jehovah, Amun got lucky.

As we have seen, he originated in Hermopolis with his twin and consor Amunet, and made the short trip up river where he supplanted Montu in the affection of the locals.

Amun, like the light in that vision of the Cord of Mut, was felt as being everywhere, but essentially unseen. Amun in fact is not a name but a title, meaning the Hidden One, or even Invisible. Esoterically he can be perceived on the same sonic levels as the sacred Om, or Aum, more effectively pronounced as *aumgn*.

According to one source, Amun came to Thebes mounted on Amunet's back, as she swam through the waters of Nun. Wherever he landed he was worshipped as the local god. As his priests were to do in earthly realms, Amun gradually usurped the roles of the other neters and took on their powers. Thus he developed the face of Ra and the form of Ptah; he lead the neters of Thebes and the Ogdoad of Hermopolis; he became linked with Min, Hapi, Montu and Harsaphes; like Osiris he was a Horned God beloved of the common people. In truth he became all things to all people as creatures from the astral levels can. Although he took over as his own the sophisticated aspects of Ptah as an all-pervasive energy, he appealed to the simpler folk as the ithyphallic man with skin like lapis-lazuli, or else in those bull or ram-headed roles which linked him with the earlier fertility cults. In relation to the latter, one of the tales about Amun describes how he once disguised himself in the skin of a flayed and beheaded ram - an image which has clear echoes of the original shamanism.

As far as priests seeking temporal power were concerned, Amun was quite literally a god-send.

★

Amun was associated with the Nile Goose as an aspect of the Great Cackler, whose egg magically parallels that egg within the woman which when fertilised by the sperm cell, eventually produces a baby growing in the womb. The sperm cells themselves have parallels in those swarming, writhing and frog-spawning creatures of the Ogdoad from which Amun emerged. The Ancient Egyptians had no need for the techniques of modern microscopy to be able to discern these functions: when the Sem is properly connected with the neters, as they function on all levels of existence, the symbolism which comes through is consistent throughout.

Another image - far more important - was that of the ram, whose great sexual vigour gifted Amun the title 'Lord of the Two Horns', and enabled him to match and rival the Cult of Osiris.

He also bore the title of Amun Kem-Atef in his role as a primordial serpent, this meaning 'he who has completed his moment', or even (once again) the 'ever-becoming one'. In this case it alludes to the snake shedding his old skin and beginning again with another. In human terms we Travellers do this too, at various stages in our lives. We also become Amun Kem-Atef.

This particular title is also the origin of Kneph, a self-begotten divinity who is almost the masculine answer to Mut in her role as the self-fertilising vulture. Kneph's role refers to the idea of the serpent swallowing its tail, a universal image of the androgyne, of Male-Female achieving their alchemical union. Kneph was the common man's attempt to resolve the elusiveness of the Hidden One, and give him something of the air of Hero, too. At the same time, with his impartial sense of justice which favoured neither high nor low, he was also given the role of 'vizier of the poor'.

All things to all men, all things to all women - all and everything, that was Amun. While at his most esoteric levels he was described as being the *ba* of Geb and the *ba* of Osiris. Whether this was yet more priestly aggrandisement or accurate assessment is a matter for the devotee.

★

Amun may be the Hidden One but he can be found, easily enough in a variety of ways.

Whenever we feel a pleasing breeze upon our skin, then that is Amun. The air and its winds, breezes and gales may be invisible in itself, but can discerned in its effects. Amun makes clouds race, corn bend, and skin tingle. It was quite clear that without air the life of mammals could not be sustained. Amun was felt in the air. And if anyone was foolish enough to hold their breath beyond normal limits, trapping the air within, then they would turn the colour of lapis lazuli - which was Amun all over. At the same time crude folk of all classes would have their little jokes about farting which involved arch-references to the Hidden One, and his mysterious ways. The savants meanwhile postulated on his links with Shu, the primordial spirit of the air. Barren women would stand naked at his sacred places and assume the *ka* posture and hope that the pressures of Amun would help with their fertility, releasing those hormones which would stimulate the ovary to start ripening an egg in anticipation.

We can find Amun, also, when we lie flat upon the ground and become aware of our own weight, as it is affected by gravity. By a shift of the mind it is possible to imagine that the weight we feel is not our own pressing upon the ground, but the earth's weight pressing upward on us. This is when we get close to Amun as the *ba* of Geb, or else in his role as Amun-Min. Vaguely erotic feelings can accompany this exercise; if we follow them, we can get close to the very essence of magic.

And then there are the ram-aspects of Amun which we can glimpse when we meet a physically desirable person and say under our breath: *Mmmmnn...*

With a bit of ingenuity we can find the Hidden One in so many places that he almost becomes the Obvious One if we get too arrogant about it. When that happens, however, we lose him completely.

★

Thebes is the place of the Moon, of the ovaries or testes, the uterus, and those hormones which ensure that we are able to carry life forward. It is when the nucleus of the sperm fuses with the nucleus of the egg that the genes, or unit of inheritance of the two parents meet. On our spiritual voyage towards a more permanent kind of Union, the nucleus of the present can fuse with the nucleus of the past, and give shape to the future of both the individual Traveller, and that of his people. In the womb, that 'Empty Room' which is the focus of all the goddess temples, all embryos start off being female and are only gradually turned into males if there is a Y chromosome. Men are simply women with male hormones added. Amunet/Mut is the norm, the source. Amun comes later.

Amun came down from Hermopolis with his twin and consort Amunet. In another sense this means that when an individual has ordered and controlled his world by means of his 'fight or flight' adrenaline responses, he can begin to think about reproducing himself. Survival first and then perpetuation. Hermopolis and then Thebes.

Amun rode across Nun on Amunet's back - the woman carrying the man through Chaos, in an image that holds no mysteries for any female.

At Thebes Amunet became as omnipresent and adept at shape-shifting as her consort, taking on the primary form of Mut. As a mother she needed a firm image, which also provided a firm womb for the ideas that she brought to birth.

Mut, in turn, became closely linked with Sekhmet, and we might regard one as the *ba* of the other. Which way around is purely a matter of preference. Mut and Sekhmet themselves have never worried too much about notions of precedence.

It was within the Precinct of Mut that Amun was worshipped in his serpent-form of Amun Kem-Atef. This was Mut's purest consort, the Vulture and the Serpent combining in symbol that is redolent of the Upper and Lower Kingdoms. Mut as a vulture could get pregnant by opening her wings to the wind and soaring toward the sun. The serpent pushed its way across the earth or through water. When they united so did the Elements. Both serpent and vulture laid eggs from which life emerged - which once again hearkens back to the Great Cackler or Hermopolis.

Mut/Amunet carries Amun within her. The Hidden One becomes a symbol of every woman's potential for giving birth, and bringing new phases of consciousness into the world. Mut/Amunet is that which brings form and stability out of nothingness.

★

Just as the ovaries and testes can produce hormones responsible for the secondary sexual characteristics, so does the Thebes-influence exert itself upon the religious impulses in terms of matriarchal or patriarchal tendencies. Clearly the whole notion of gods and goddesses and why one sex gained dominance within a religion or a culture at any given time, is a massive topic for debate. In our present Journey the Traveller can go toward those images which best appeal to his or her own tendencies. Khem's pantheons are vast enough to cater for all tastes, all sexist passions. In Thebes, however, in the Precinct of Mut, we must concentrate upon the women.

★

When it comes to looking at the role of women within the temples, rather than at the womb as a temple in itself, it has to be admitted that very little acknowledged reference has survived about the activities of the priestesses, even though women in Khem had rights and a status which would be envied by their sisters in many so-called 'modern' European nations today.

Orthodox Egyptologists assume that all the priestesses did was shake their sistra and sing hymns before the statues of the neters, because they bore the sacerdotal titles 'Singers' and 'Musicians', and were also dancers. In fact they did to the souls of the departed what modern, popular singers now do to mass audiences: they used the powers of song and personal magnetism to bring life, light and love and a bit more than that into areas of consciousness that were previously dead or dormant. They could sing the souls up from the Duat, calling them into the world - if only briefly. Hollywood might have seen its true origins in Khem, but the best of the modern, female, pop or rock or soul singers would have been quite at home among the priestesses.

★

The ladies started coming into their own during the 20th Dynasty when Egypt was experiencing one of those troubled times when the central authority had broken down - yet again. The great days of Rameses II were long over. The empire that Egypt once had was just a memory, and all she retained was Nubia. The many Rameses who followed the II were no comparison to their fabled namesake. And all the while that these later kings struggled to assert themselves, the priests of Amun were slowly, discreetly, but very surely undermining everything they tried to do.

We can see the same thing happening to adolescents, and we have experienced it ourselves: no matter what noble thoughts or impulses we might have are coloured or often swept away entirely by the burgeoning feelings and compulsions of our sexuality. In Khem the pharaoh no longer kept his court in Thebes, but in the delta at Tanis. Quite simply they could not contend with the growing power of the Theban priesthood. To a great degree it happens in every nation, as the structures of adoration and support become greater than the focus. In time, pharaoh's only curb upon the priesthood was to be able to name his own High Priest. Even this back-fired however, as by the time that Rameses IX selected a man named Amenhotep to be his High Priest in Thebes, the situation was so out of control that Amenhotep could have himself depicted on the walls of Theban temples the same size as Pharaoh - an unheard of move in the world of the neters and their representatives, but universally known when the adolescent male (knowing everything) challenges his own father. Yet it meant, in effect, that Amenhotep was now the ruler of Thebes, and thus the whole of Upper Egypt.

By the time that the eleventh Rameses ruled in Tanis the system in Thebes had become so audacious that Rameses XI's nominee, Herihor, had himself depicted as Pharaoh with the full and incantatory titles: Horus, Strong Bull Son-of-Amun, King of Upper and Lower Egypt, Lord of the Two Lands, First Prophet of Amun, Bodily Son of Ra, Son-of-Amun, Herihor.

The whole system became so outrageous, so unbalanced, that somehow and in some way it needed Woman to step in and assume equal amounts of power over a long period in order to go some way to restoring the religious balances. In fact it was actually Herihor who created the opening, because he began a system of what might be called 'religio-political' marriages and alliances which was to change the whole structure of Khem for quite some time. After the fall of the 20th Dynasty, Thebes was ruled almost exclusively by the high-priests of Amun. But from the time of Osorkon III of the 23rd Dynasty to that of Psamtik III of the 26th, Thebes was governed by a succession of five 'God's Wives of Amun', whose names we might give now as Shepenwepe I, Amonortais I, Shepenwepe II, Nitocris, and Ankhnesneferibre.

Originally the title 'God's Wife' of Amun' was given to the pharaoh's spouse, but by the time of the 22nd Dynasty this title was transferred to the king's daughter, who became the consecrated wife of the god himself, whom no mortal may sully. At least this was the principle, for at least one God's Wife, name of Makare, the daughter of Psusennes I, had a child which was buried next to her in her tomb. Proof indeed that sometimes the 'Theban' urges toward giving life were too powerful even for the highest of priestesses.

By the time of the 25th and 26th Dynasties, during the Ethiopian supremacy, the God's Wife was appointed as a deliberately political act which often involved the notion of adoption. Thus Koshtu gave his daughter Amonortais I to be adopted by Shepenwepe I, who was herself a daughter of the last of the Bubastite kings. This same Amonortais I later became an adoptive mother herself to Shepenwepe the daughter of King Pi'ankhy.

When these women ruled Thebes as effective High Priestesses, they were to all intents and purposes the equal of the king himself, with lands and officials of their own, enormous wealth and absolute prestige. What was technically their male counterpart and

Figure 25 - Princess Amenarteis

equal, the High Priest of Amun in Thebes, was little more than a shadow under the rule of each. It was the period in Khem's history when Amunet, wearied with the masculine mis-use of Amun's power, decided to remind the nation just where the true sources of their vitality really lay... within the woman. In fact the only real limitation on the God's Wife's authority was that she was confined to Thebes, and Thebes alone. This is a testament to the womb and limited confines giving birth to all life in so many areas, but putting definite restrictions upon the mother in others.

< Figure 26a - Ankhnesneferibre

Figure 26b - Queen Karoma >

It was the Nubians who took this idea of the God's Wife back into their own country and, during the Roman period when Egypt had become that nation's bread basket, produced a line of Nubian queens at Meroe and Napata who gave many great and grave problems to Egypt's overlords. These Nubian queens even called themselves the 'Daughters of Amun' in a later echo of the God's Wives.

★

We can make acknowledgements to these powerful women in the Precinct of Mut if we wish, but their main response will always be toward the company of women. Men they knew in plenty and often rather scorned; it is with women that they will share glimpses of their glorious careers, suggesting similar possibilities within the lives of the female Traveller. In the Precinct of Mut, men should bide their time and keep very very quiet. And all such contacts should be made via the Lady Tui in any case. Not everyone gets past her.

★

All temples had priestesses attached them, usually in a separate and specific area. Many of them were 'musician priestesses' called 'hnwt' or 'hnyt' (pronounced as henut and henit respectively), although from the New Kingdom onwards the title became 'sm'wt', pronounced as shem.ut. Often, like the men, they were just called we'ebs. It was a position that was open to women of all classes, high or low, and acceptance was based less upon a musical aptitude with the sistrum, but on whether or not they had a 'feel' for the particular neters with which the temple was involved. Many of them were given the opportunity for further training which would enable them to become prophetesses, which involved far more in the way of magical work, and took them closer to the very heart of the mysteries. One such prophetess, Neshkons, who was the wife of Pinudjem II, bore on her coffin the legend:

> 'First chief of the concubines of Amun-Ra, King of the Gods; major-domo of the house of Mut the great, lady of Isheru; prophetess of Anhur-Shu the son of Ra, prophetess of Min, Horus and Isis in Akhmin, prophetess of Horus, the lord of Djuef, god's mother of Khonsu the Child, first one of Amun-Ra, King of the Gods, and chief of noble ladies.'

Neshkons can come to us in the Precinct of Mut, which she knew and loved. If the present female reader who has not yet become a

Traveller might care to make Neshkons' contact here at Thebes first, then she could do worse than make her Journey with such a prophetess in the stern.

★

One thing every priestess knew was that even though their lives were consecrated to a particular goddess, they were equally involved with that figure's consort. And conversely so for the priests, of course. A man can channel Mut as effectively (though in a different way) as any woman. Women were not called Concubines of Amun out of sexist dominance, but because they could enter into magical, sensual relationships with that god, and with the spirit of Life itself. Energies would flow back and forth between the worlds which were directly analogous to human intercourse. Women *and* men in touch with their neters could involve them in their own reproductive processes to help bring a Moonchild into the world - though this was not necessarily a physical child.

Much of this arcanum lies within our own hands, as we move slowly about the Precinct of Mut still clutching the *uas* wand that Kha'm-uast handed on to us. Before we go on to call up Khonsu, and bring our Journey to a close, we really have to study this implement in a little more detail.

★

The Traveller can, on any future expedition through the inner levels of Khem, use the *uas* wand as a kind of lodestone: suspended before the mind's eye by the gleaming thread of consciousness, it will point the way to whichever power sources will offer the greatest opportunities for wisdom.

The word *uas* means simply 'sceptre', and the *uas* wand can be regarded as a schematic design for the flow of the magical currents as they course up the spine. The head of the *uas* wand shows how the currents exit via the brow, or the ajna chakra, and also the crown of the head - the sahasrara chakra. The central point of the *uas* wand's head, indicates that mid-brain source of ancient consciousness and experience which was the true starting-point of the Journey. The shaft of the wand matches the length of the individual's backbone, while the twin ends at the base indicate those currents which twine upwards like serpents - the ida and pingala of the Hindu traditions, and the Two Ways of the Egyptian. The two ends also depict the dualities that are found throughout the symbolism of Egyptian religion: Male and Female principles uniting in a single upsurge of consciousness which develops itself into that head-shape which is always associated with Set.

~ 152 ~

Although the image of the ankh has taken on popular appeal to such an extent that it is now almost a universal symbol, the *uas* is no less important.

The *uas* wand is the prime symbol of the vertebrate in control of its environment, with all of the positive and negative energies in harness, and all rising to consciousness in the form of Set. Which alludes to the perennial occult secrets which every occultist has heard, but which seems to be whispered afresh for every generation: that the *true* lord of this world is Set/Seth/Satan. In other aspects this is Lucifer, the lightbearer, who was banished from heaven because he would not acknowledge the newly-created Mankind ahead of his Creator. Banished from heaven because he loved too much, he was made to rule over Matter until such a time as Matter transcends itself again, and Malkuth rejoins Daath, and Man climbs toward the angels again.

In even more obscure areas of magic, Set was the original Slayer. This is not meant in the sense of random murder, but in the sense of Set as the Sacrificial Priest who slays the Divine King when his time has come. In this sense some of Set's priests argue still that he was the true heir to Osiris' throne, the next true avatar of Geb, the Earth God. They argue that he was cheated by Isis' act of giving birth to an heir long after Osiris died.

But although Set was forever placed as a supporter of the solar barque in its journey through the Duat, his followers have secretly looked forward to the time when Anubis will satisfy all factions and take over the reins of the next Aeon.

All of which may seem a far cry from our stop at Thebes, but in fact the lodestone formed by our suspended *uas* necessarily spins around wildly like compass needles do at the North Pole, for the symbol finds its source at Thebes, or Uas, the Greek name Thebai being a corruption of Ta-ope, which was an ancient name for Luxor. The sceptre, or symbol of royal authority, was usually handed down through the generations as a symbol of what might be termed 'genetic authority', or 'blood royal' - the union of two chosen opposites to create qualities which could be passed on to the next generation. On top of that the *uas* wand is the perfect expression of the Wand of Power which features so largely in all ancient and modern magic.

And so Thebes *was* power, in all of its manifestations, with all of its rights and wrongs.

★

It has long been a belief among Gnostics and Dualists generally that Hell was - quite literally - here on Earth. It was a philosophy which found its most exotic expressions amid the flowering of Alexandria but which was certainly discussed in the earlier mystery centres. In this respect there are indications that the Duat, through which we have endeavoured to travel, was actually here on Earth also. Not so much an underworld beneath our feet (in literal and figurative senses), but the actual earth on which we stand. This is the 'underworld' in the sense that we live here under those celestial realms which are the true home of the gods.

Like the kabbalistic sphere of Daath (and there may be etymological links here) which can be regarded as 'inner earth', the Duat is linked with the earth-realm via the subconscious links that we make between the actual land, and something greater than ourselves. Thus anyone who can stand at a particular site and feel a sense of dread and delight, fear or rapture, will be in touch with the Duat. Somewhere in this geographical area, which responds to an area within the individual's psyche, there will be 'gates' linking the energies of the Traveller with the energies 'beneath' the land on which he stands. For the Traveller in question the site will become his own version of 'God's little acre' - or in this case, using an Egyptian term of reference, 'The Gods' little aker'. If the Traveller feels no response to the site or locale, then there will be no Gates, no access to the Duat from there, for him or her at least. Wherever and whenever we can feel a response, however, there we are close to Thebes, close to 𓊽

★

Where we are born, where we live, or where we find ourselves at particularly important moments in our lives, is motivated less by the stars above than by the telluric energies beneath. Like those writhing red and black dragons of alchemy (and also Upper and Lower Egypt) we can use these subterranean energies to rise toward the pure gold of Set, whose name is actually punningly similar to the Egyptian word for that precious metal. According to the arts of alchemy, pure gold is to be found within the inner structures of lead, the heaviest metal: while on another level, the transforming powers of Set are to be extracted from the densest of matter.

★

Kha'm-uast, then, retained his name meaning 'Manifestation in Thebes' because it was a statement of his place within the scheme.

Uas, as we have seen, refers to Thebes.

'm simply means 'in'   𓏞 𓅓 𓊽

While Kha is another of the insubstantial parts of the occult anatomy - not to be confused with the *ka*.

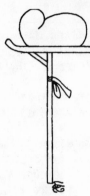

The kha was especially associated with the concept of royalty. It was something in the nature of an 'external soul' which we might equate with a national identity, or figurehead like Brittania or Uncle Sam. It was regarded as residing in the placenta or umbilical cord. At the birth of a prince, especially one destined as future king, the placenta and/or umbilical cord was dried and preserved, then carefully bound up in special wrappings or a container. The wrappings/container was called the 'Bundle of Life', and were fixed upon a standard that was always carried in procession before the king, elevated toward the sky to indicate that pharaoh still acknowledged his links with that source.

From the time of the Scorpion-King until the Ptolemys the placenta standard was always paraded.

The custom was begun of appointing 'Guardians of the Royal Placenta', a title which Kha'm-uast claimed on his Image for Eternity. One Egyptological scholar speculated that while kings in Egypt may have been ritually slaughtered once they were past their prime, by dynastic times a different system had arisen. This was where the role of Guardian/Opener of the Royal Placenta was instituted, and the Opener in pre-dynastic times was actually charged with the task of the ritual murder.

'The executioner was often a man of the highest rank...the 'Opener of the Royal Placenta'. In any explanation of the custom of king-killing, it must be borne in mind that in primitive times the executioner would most probably be the next successor to the throne. This would account for the fact that in the Old Kingdom the 'Opener' was nearly always related to the King by blood or marriage. The custom of killing the King had probably changed before the Old Kingdom to the sacrifice of a vicarious victim, but the ceremony of opening the Bundle of Life might very well take place at the death of the substitute, and the King's won life would then be renewed by binding it again in the Bundle after the sacrifice. The 5th Dynasty still remembered the custom of putting the King to death, as the Texts of Pepy and Meren-Ra (Pyramid Texts 1453-4) show; and it is also evident that the custom belonged to the primitive stratum of the religion of which the god Seth was the deity, an earlier stratum than the Osiris cult.'*

It is a curious thing that the authority just quoted was Dr Margaret Murray, whose books of witchcraft and the cult of the Divine King in Europe went no small way to resurrecting the Craft and giving it an historical basis.

It is hardly surprising that Kha'm-uast, who was the inner contact behind certain pagan currents of this century, should also appear in this context.

The Opener of the Royal Placenta later became known as its Guardian, and his role as executioner of the king was more directed toward the Apis Bulls than the king himself. Because the religion of Osiris placed emphasis on rebirth and renewal, this concept was incorporated into the ceremonies connected with the Bundle of Life, as a direct complement to the Opening of the Mouth ceremonies, and tied in with the Heb-Sed festival, the time of renewal for kings, and the reassumption of royal duties.

And beneath it all was Set.

And the one who wove inbetween all the strands of all the cults was Anubis, in his roles as Opener of the Way and Guardian.

He never forgot his fathers - either of them. One way or another he will satisfy them both.

And it is through him, as we take on Kha'm-uast's qualities for ourselves, that we will bring the Aeon through.

*

Much of these particular mysteries can be resolved and yet at the same time magnified by the image of the *shedshed*, a mystic staff which is almost a summation of all that has gone before: the djed, symbol of the backbone and stability, and the tree in which Osiris was entrapped; the ankh, symbol of Isis' womb or vagina, depending upon context; the basal fork representing the dualities of life on earth; the small ankh emerging from head of the uas, which in itself emerges from the larger ankh, as if being born.

The shedshed, when brooded upon, becomes a disturbingly potent symbol with facility for keeping the meditator awake at nights. The answer to the question 'How do you understand life on earth' can be answered by every individual's interpretation of this staff.

---

* Margaret Murray, "The Bundle of Life," from *Ancient Egypt*, March 1930, p.71.

Traditionally it was linked with the royal placenta, and was regarded as the emblem on which pharaoh rose to the heavens. In each case the king was always shown in the guise of Wepwawet when he held it, emphasising the sanctity of his blood-line, and 'opening the way' into and out of life for the rest of us.

★

In the Precinct of the Vulture, however, Mut has little interest in any details of the Dark Son or Black Dog when her own child is there to be adored. If the Priestesses of Mut necessarily work with Amun also, then by the same token they can scarcely avoid Khonsu.

Khonsu was known as the Wanderer, the Traveller, and even as the Navigator. Within these titles alone we can see distinct links with our own Journey. In his case the wandering, travelling and navigating all related to the path of the moon across the sky: in our case it involves building a road through the subconscious.

He was also known and worshipped as Khonsu-peh-Khered, which is simply Khonsu the Child. In this aspect he also had mysterious links with the human placenta, and its umbilical cord, the former seen as a parallel of the moon within, the latter as the way in which we link with it.

He is often shown in human form wearing a garment that does not allow his limbs to be differentiated; sometimes he is shown hawk-headed, wearing the lunar disk between the horns of the crescent moon. He was a god of fertility, conception, and childbirth. One of his sacred animals was the baboon, which shows that he too has strong connections with Hermopolis.

At certain festivals his statue was magically charged and transported in his own sacred boat to join the statues of his parents in the temple of Luxor, and so complete the sacred Triad of Thebes. Such a ritual may have seemed ridiculous at the beginning of our own Journey, but it must, surely, take on a curious kind of sense in these final stages.

Khonsu, in Thebes at least, was regarded as that within us which controls our destiny. This aspect was known as Khonsu Heseb Ahau, the 'Reckoner of the life-span' - and much more besides.

We have already seen how the Theban Triad closely parallels that of Memphis. We might begin by looking at Khonsu in the light of Nefertum.

The latter was (and is) the spirit of the Bright Idea. He comes through to us via scientific formulae, via all the different 'istics' and 'ologies', the concepts of line, form and ratio, and all those ideas as hard and sharp as tungsten cutting tools.

In contrast Khonsu brings us all the dreams under the moon; of dungeons and dragons, lost continents, giants who walked the earth, secret temples, and Sirius and Venus and animal-headed humans, and men with wings or one eye in the centre of the brow, and elves and gnomes and all those images from the dream-time of the Earth's consciousness. All of them are fairy-tales, in essence. They may or may not have literal truths within them, but it is the spirit of the telling which contains the power. Just as loving parents can recapture the lost and earliest years of their own childhoods by observing their own children, so can we glimpse the near-forgotten 'demi-paradise' of the Earth's beginnings through Khonsu.

Nefertum developed an avatar in the form of Imhotep, who became deified in the former's place, assuming the same qualities.

Khonsu never developed similar during his long history in Khem, but he has often pressed hard to do so today, here in the West. In guardedly Wiccan terms the Field (ley) of the Crow can lead us into the same areas as the invocations to Khonsu in the Precinct of the Vulture. The image of the priest carrying the Ape of Thoth can help in this respect also.

In the short lives that we lead we must look to Khonsu to gain some control over our own destinies. In so doing we learn the full magic of the moon, which acts toward our consciousness as the placenta does toward the foetus. All Travellers who are unclear about the latter should make their own efforts to find out and relate the two. This individual effort is one of the secrets of the *uas*. Without it, we will never explore the secrets of Thebes, or anywhere else for that matter.

★

Very often in our dreams we work out the alternative possibilities of paths we could have, or should have taken in our lives but did not. At a certain point in magical work these alternative possibilities can flow through our dream-life with an often disturbing intensity, although they eventually discharge themselves.

At the same time, when the power of the *uas* wand becomes ingrained within the individual's psyche, he finds that he becomes subject to a kind of 'instant karma'. Unbalanced, unfair and injudicious acts will tend to rebound instantly, leaving no possibility that any such accumulated energies might impede his progress in the near future. In nautical terms he comes to see his own bow-wave being formed, and watches where it goes, and sees the wash coming back to him from the sides of the small pond in which he floats.

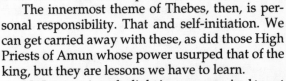

The innermost theme of Thebes, then, is personal responsibility. That and self-initiation. We can get carried away with these, as did those High Priests of Amun whose power usurped that of the king, but they are lessons we have to learn.

No Journey into the light is ever easy. And to get there we have to approach it with Khonsu.

The place that we must aim to reach, now that we are almost qualified Travellers, is the womb. In the scheme of the neters this exists on numerous levels of understanding and actuality: the physical womb of our own mother; the womb of the subconscious through which our body of light travels; the womb of the Great Mother in which we all exist, forever and ever, Amun.

At this point in Thebes, still within the Precinct of Mut, still holding the *uas* wand or even the *shedshed*, if we can cope with it, we must create a sequence of intense imagery which will get us into one of these.

We can do so by placing ourselves at the sacred lake's edge again, at the place where Khonsu's navel would be. Or we can place ourselves in the bare, pure Temple of Khonsu the Child at the northeast corner of the enclosure. Or we can enter the Temple of Mut itself if it calls. Or we can - best of all - use none of these, and create something completely original, and become like Kneph, all self-created and creative in all things .

We must enter the moon along the beam of light; we must touch the placenta which once gave us our entire nourishment; we must float like a star in the amniotic waters (the Nun) of the Great Mother.

However we manage this state we should precede it by a review of all those particular decisions made in the past which have brought us to our present point in life, tracking them backwards through our memory. The decisions concerned are not necessarily the major ones of life, death, marriage, mortgage or pension-funds, but often those apparently tiny moments which, in retrospect, altered all things. For example, choosing job A instead of job B; choosing lover A instead of lover B; failing to beat-up the class bully when you had a brief and reasonably good chance...and so on. All those choices/paths which you did *not* take are the ones that will work themselves out through dreams. Sometimes they may actually loop around into your life again, at a much later date.

This is clearly by no means an easy exercise in simple reverie. Then again, there is nothing easy about the energies in the *uas* wand. Even as the Traveller starts to track back through them, in reverse order, new ones can spring up which have to be caught and hung out to dry like the small fish near the prow of the Henu Boat. Sometimes, with memories such as these, the best thing to do in the long run is to gut, fillet and consume them. And there is another useful scenario for the Traveller there if he is resourceful enough.

What we are aiming at, eventually, is to enter those misty years of childhood before our conscious memories firmed, pushing our visualisation back until we can actually enter the womb in some symbolic way, and find ourselves afloat in the waters, knowing the stillness and hearing the blood flowing around, and hearing that heart pumping it which contains all the life in the world.

We become like the embryonic Khonsu at this point, floating like an astronaut in space, secure within our life-support system. We become feeble and helpless, and yet we represent a fusion of two fully conscious adults, and all the adults in their bloodlines too.

Floating in the womb, acutely aware (via the umbilical cord and placenta) of being connected to some all-encompassing source of life and nourishment beyond yourself, can be a powerful and moving experience: the disasters and desperations of life have not yet happened; all the possibilities are in front of you and the pattern to manipulate them within you.

In fact it is here, via the umbilical and placenta, that we find the *kha*, which is said to reside in them. This is the same *kha* as in Kha'm-uast. Although the word has been translated as 'Manifesta-tion', it can be extended to mean 'glimmering' or 'dawning' - an anticipation of light, rather than light itself. In fact it is a radiance which we create for ourselves. Things begin to dawn, light begins to rise, whenever we make any efforts, any *original* attempts to re-turn to the Source. It does not matter how crass or absurd these efforts may seem to anyone else, it does not matter what imagery or belief-systems are used - as long as the work done is original then the link between the would-be initiate and the primary moon-consciousness will be forged. The dawning of the light, the glimmering of the *kha*, will start to make itself apparent; the *uas* wand will be sealed into the psyche.

It is in this sense that every Traveller becomes, at this point, within Thebes, Kha'm-uast in his own right. It is in this sense that Kha'm-uast is a potential within us all, quite apart from a separate and historical individual.

★

This particular exercise is not finished yet, however. The Traveller can actually attempt to go back even further, to the years before he manifested himself in matter, when he was laying down certain patterns for the life to come. He can do so by visualising the umbilical cord as a great vortex whirling before him - much like that spiritual vortex which is said to attract souls into incarnation in the first place. In fact they are one and the same, but functioning in different directions.

When this exercise really 'takes', it is almost impossible to describe, even in the most symbolic of terms. But even if the greater intensity of the experience is lacking, and the Traveller feels that he is doing no more than going through some imagined motions, it still can be used with great effect. He can re-run the major stages of his life up until the present, and then push on into his future, setting down those images of himself and his life that he would want to see happen: greater strength, greater tolerance, an end to bad luck or illness... if destiny is partly, largely, or wholly a matter of character, or *ka*, then he effectively re-patterns himself for the sake of his own future. The Traveller should visualise all this as intensely as possible, even if he feels that he is, in a sense, wrestling with the gods of his fate. He could also use the glyph of the sekhem which means 'image', and plant it in the ground next to the future scenes he builds up, perhaps with the appropriate year clearly marked on it to indicate when he wants this to occur.  From the Waters of Nun in which he finds himself, he should insist to the neters that this will be so.

This is the magician taking control of his own life and world. This is the Traveller becoming responsible for his own light.

This is an exercise which can have very real though not

immediately obvious effects. Like all things, it will work to a greater or lesser extent depending upon the efforts of the individual. Yet even if it did not work, at least at the end of our lives we will be able to tell our grandchildren about the period we attempted to sail through Time and into the secret heart of Khem in company with a High Priest of Ptah to wrestle with our destinies. At very least we will have proved to the world to come that we have a 'strong *ka*' and were never just spiritual drifters. In our own Image for Eternity, such as that laid down by Kha'm-uast in Abydos, or around his 'false door' at the Serapeum, we will be able to name ourselves as 'Such-and-Such, Traveller, Justified'.

That alone is something that few people in this world can claim.

*

All of which effectively brings us to the end of our present Journey as we hover here at our own Source, bearing the title Kha'm-uast as ours by right of travel, and effort. What began as the merest impulse in the primitive centre of the mid-brain ends in an act of self-creation at Thebes, the effectiveness of which will depend entirely upon the heart and will of the individual.

Just as the placenta is able to separate the baby's blood from that of the mother, so can we link ourselves with a neter without losing our individuality. As the placenta, or the Theban 'moon-magic' starts to function, it gradually takes over responsibility for producing a range of hormones, including oestrogen and progesterone, from those endocrine glands which normally secrete them. And so we feel ourselves linked, despite our individuality, with something greater than ourselves, and in tune with the neters. At the same time as we 'conceive' Khonsu within us, we also become Khonsu ourselves. Worlds within worlds, minds within minds, matter and spirit become One. All those who practise magic at Thebes become moon children.

In each case, after each exercise, the Traveller really should make efforts to 'close down' whatever psychic faculties have been stimulated. If they have come so far on the Journey they will almost certainly have their own ideas as to how this may be done. As mentioned earlier, this can involve a simple gesture in which doors are felt as closing on the brow; or the body visualised as being swathed in lead bandages; the Nile can be seen to retreat beyond the mouth of Khebit's harbour; the Henu Boat felt as settling back into its sledge; or the Traveller can simply use the symbol of the Duat, the ⊗ , as a door through which they can step back into normality.

This may well leave us with the curious sense of melancholy that all Travellers feel at the end of any stimulating travel; a sense that there should be more, coupled with the eternal feeling that no person can ever really return home once they have left it. In regard to Khem itself there is still a vast and inexhaustible range of places to visit, neters to work with, as even the most casual knowledge of that realm will reveal. The Traveller does not even need the Henu Boat to explore them, nor yet have to accept any of the parallels and analyses given herein. By means of heart and will, and any original effort, he can rise like Osiris, upward to his own light and his own perception of Khem - or any other realm for that matter.

★

And so we have manifested ourselves at Thebes and started to take control, and set foot upon the long path towards becoming a Sem. We have also, in forming our own exercises within the Precinct of Mut, started those embryonic twitchings in the womb of the Great Mother which tells her that we are at last alive within. Only at our physical deaths will she actually give birth to us in the fullest sense.

We could now link all the centres in one simple *ka* ritual and the best place to stand as we do so is between the pillars of the northern gate (and only gate) of Mut's Precinct, facing down the long, long avenue of ram-headed sphinxes, looking toward the Great Temple of Amun, and beyond that (with a visionary eye) to the length and breadth of the Upper and Lower Kingdoms, and the rippling currents of the Nile which now flows in your own direction.

With the Lady Tui's hands upon your shoulders from behind, the *uas* wand in your own grasp, and the potential of the Henu Boat anywhere you need it to manifest, and in any form, a whole realm awaits you, and the end of the Journey becomes no more than another beginning.

As they said in Thebes: start with the Moon, and the rest will slowly, slowly, happen...

Khemnu priest with his baboon

APPENDIX

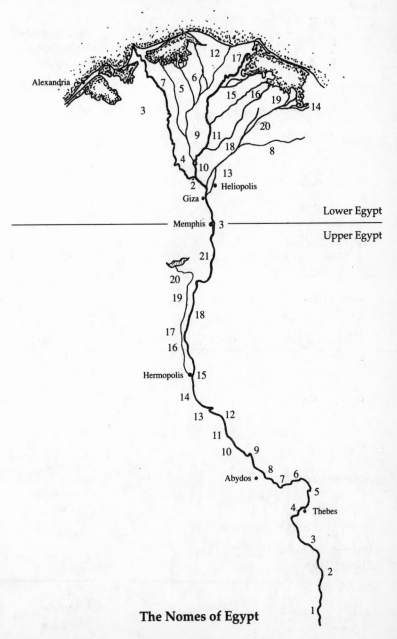

The Nomes of Egypt

The Nome Symbols of Lower Egypt

Symbol and Title	Associated Centres	Deities
White Walls	Memphis, Saqqara, Abusir	Ptah, Seknmet Nefertum, Sokar, Api
Foreleg	Letopolis	Horus
West	Damanhur, Kom el-Hisn	Hathor
Southern Shield		Neith
Northern Shield	Buto, Chemmis	Neith, Isis, the infant Horus
Mountain Bull 	Xois	Ra
Western Harpoon 		Ha
Eastern Harpoon	Pithom	Atum-Ra

Symbol and Title	Associated Centres	Deities
Andjety	Busiris	Osiris
Black Ox	Athribis	Horus
Ox-count	Leontopolis	Shu, Tefnut
Cow and Calf	Sebennytos	Onuris
Inviolate Sceptre	Heliopolois	Atum, Iusaas, Nu, Geb
Foremost of the East	Pelusium	Set-Typhon
Ibis	Mendes	Thoth

Symbol and Title	Associated Centres	Deities

Fish

Behdet

Damietta   Horus

Prince of the South

Bubastis   Bast

Prince of the North

Tanis   Uatchet

Plumed Falcon of Sopedu

The Nome Symbols of Upper Egypt

Symbol and Title	Associated Centres	Deities
Ta-Sety	Elephantine, Kom Ombo	Isis, Khnum, Horus, Sobek
Throne of Horus	Edfu	Horus
Shrine	Esna, El Kab Herakonopolis	Horus, Khnum, Neith
Sceptre	Thebes, Armant	Amun, Mut, Khonsu, Montu, Sobek
Two Falcons	Coptos	Min, Seth
Crocodile	Denderah	Hathor
Sistrum	Hiw, Diospolis, Parva	Bat
Great Land	Abydos	Khentamentiu, Osiris

Symbol and Title	Associated Centres	Deities
Min	Akhmin	Min
Cobra	Qaw el-Kebir	Seth
Seth	Shutb	Seth
Viper Mount	Deir el-Gebrawi	Anti
Upper Sycamore and Viper	Asyut	Wepwawet, Anpu
Lower Sycamore and Viper	Meir	Hathor
Hare	Hermopolis, Beni Hasan	The Ogdoad, Thoth

Symbol and Title	Associated Centres	Deities
Oryx	Men 'at Khufu, Zawyat el-Amwat	Pakhet
Jackal	Hardai	Anubis
Anti	Oxyrhyncus	Anti
Two Sceptres	El-Hiba	Seth
Southern Sycamore	Herakelopolis, El-lahun, Hawara	Heryshaf
Northern Sycamore	Maidum	Khnum
Knife		Hathor

BIBLIOGRAPHY

Baines, J. and Malek, J., *Atlas of Ancient Egypt*, Phaidon Press, Oxford, 1984.

Budge, E. A. Wallis, 'The Book of Opening the Mouth', Vol. 26 of *Egypt and Chaldea*, Kegan Paul, Trench, Trubner & Co. Ltd., London, 1909.

Clark, R. T. Rundle, *Myth and Symbol in Ancient Egypt*, Thames and Hudson Ltd., London, 1978.

Gardiner, Alan, *Egypt of the Pharaohs*, Clarendon Press, Oxford, 1961.

Gomaa, Farouk, *Chaemwese, Sohn Ramses II und Hohenpriester von Memphis*, Wiesbaden, Otto Harrassowitz, 1973.

Griffith, F. Ll., *Stories of the High Priests of Memphis*, Oxford, 1900.

Ions, Veronica, *Egyptian Mythology*, Hamlyn, Feltham, 1968.

Kitchen, K.A., *Pharaoh Triumphant: The Life and Times of Ramesses II*, Aria & Phillips, Warminster, 1982.

Murray, Margaret, 'The Bundle of Life', from *Ancient Egypt*, p.71, March 1930.

Saleh, Abdel-Aziz, *Excavations at Heliopolis: Ancient Egyptian Ounu. (The Site of Tell el-Hisn-Matariyah)*, Vol. 1, Cairo University, Cairo, 1981.

West, John Anthony, *The Traveller's Key to Ancient Egypt*, Harrap Columbus, London, 1987.

INDEX